Missouri Star

The Life and Times of Martha Ann "Mattie" (Livingston) Lykins Bingham (1824-1890)

Rose Ann Findlen

Jackson County Historical Society
Independence, Missouri
2011

§The paper used in this publication meets the minimum requirements of American National Standard for Information Sciences—Permanence of Paper for Printed Library Materials, ANSI Z39.48-1984. This book is printed on recycled paper with at least 40% post-consumer materials.

Findlen, Rose Ann (Gard) (1942-)
    Missouri Star: The Life and Times of Martha Ann "Mattie" (Livingston) Lykins Bingham (1824-1890)
        194 p.   cm.
        Includes bibliographical references and index.

        ISBN-13:   978-0974136578
        ISBN: 0-9741365-7-3

First Edition, Revised June 2011.

1. Missouri–Biography. 2. Bingham, Martha Ann "Mattie" (Livingston) Lykins, 1824-1890. 3. Lykins, Johnston, 1800-1876. 4. Bingham, George Caleb, 1811-1879. 5. Painters–Missouri–Biography. 6. Politicians–Missouri–Biography. 7. Missouri–History–Civil War, 1861-1865–Social aspects. I. Findlen, Rose Ann (Gard), (1942-). II. Title.

Published by:
Jackson County Historical Society
Independence, Missouri

ABOUT THE COVER

"The Missouri Star" is a quilt block in Barbara Brackman's book, *Borderland in Butternut and Blue: A Sampler Quilt to Recall the Civil War Along the Kansas/Missouri Border*, that honors Martha Ann "Mattie" (Livingston) Lykins Bingham, a passionate, big-hearted pioneer of Kansas City. As a young girl, Laura (Coates) Reed grew up near Johnston and Mattie Lykins in Kansas City and visited their home frequently. Reed had an opportunity to witness Mattie's approach to life and described Mattie as "whole-souled" and "liberal" in terms of her largeness of spirit. Reed's mother, Sarah (Mrs. Kersey) Coates, was Mattie's lifelong friend and equal to Mattie in intellect and social activism.

Mattie was central to the building of the Westport/City of Kansas community. The quilt is an emblem of the power of individual acts in creating a community; in that capacity, Mattie was indeed a "Missouri Star." Laura (Coates) Reed wrote:

> *The sun has such a pretty quilt*
> *Each night he goes to bed,*
> *It's made of lavender and gold,*
> *With great long stripes of red.*
> *And bordered by the softest tints*
> *Of all the shades of gray.*
> *It's put together by the sky,*
> *And quilted by the day.*

Laura Reed's poem is published in Carrie A. Hall and Rose G. Kresinger, *The Romance of the Patchwork quilt in America; in Three Parts: Part I. History and Quilt Patches. Part II. Quilts--Antique and Modern. Part III. Quilting and Quilting Designs.* (Caldwell, ID: The Caxton Printers, 1935), 97.

THE DEBUT OF TWO PREVIOUSLY UNPUBLISHED IMAGES

The photograph of Martha Lykins (on the back cover and on page 19) was taken during her early days in Kansas City, in 1865, by S. M. Eby & Son, Kansas City Ambrotype and Photographic Artists. It debuts in *Missouri Star* through the generosity of Robert Dewit Owen, Mattie's great-great grandnephew, who donated the original to the Jackson County Historical Society in March 2011.

The oil portrait (in the upper right corner of the front cover and on page 105) is currently identified as "An Unknown Woman," and is purportedly the long-lost George Caleb Bingham painting of his third wife, Martha Ann "Mattie" (Livingston) Lykins Bingham, titled, *Mrs. General Bingham*.

TABLE OF CONTENTS

A CHRONOLOGY

Martha Ann "Mattie"
(Livingston) Lykins Bingham

1800	Birth of **Johnston Lykins** in Virginia
1811	Birth of **George Caleb Bingham**
1822	Baptism of **Johnston Lykins** by **Isaac McCoy** at mission in Michigan
1824	Birth of **Martha Ann "Mattie" Livingston** in Shelbyville, Shelby County, Kentucky (January)
ca. 1826	Death of **Martha (Jackson) Livingston**, Mattie's mother
ca. 1828	Death of **Stephen Livingston**, Mattie's father
1828	Removal of Wea, Piankeshaw, and Shawnee Native American nations to Kansas Territory
1828	Settlement of **Johnston and Delilah McCoy Lykins** and children at Shawnee Baptist Mission in Kansas Territory
abt. 1828-1838	**Mattie's** childhood with grandmother (likely **Sarah Livingston**, in Frankfort, Kentucky)

ca. 1838-1842	Mattie's years with **William Wooten Owen** and sister, **Elizabeth Owen**, in Shelby County, Kentucky
1836	Marriage of **George Caleb Bingham** to **Sarah Elizabeth Hutchinson** (April 14)
1840	Publication of *The Forest Cottage*, **Mattie's** novelette in *Shelby News*
1840-47	**Mattie's** years living alternately with two sisters
1841	**Johnston Lykins'** publication of first Indian language newspaper/first newspaper in Kansas Territory
1842	**Mattie's** move to Missouri with sister, **Rebecca Hughes**
1844	Death **of Delilah (McCoy) Lykins,** Johnston Lykins' first wife
1847	**Mattie's** move to Lexington, Kentucky, to open school for girls
1848	Death of **Sarah Elizabeth (Hutchinson) Bingham, George Caleb Bingham's** first wife (November 24)
1849	Marriage of **George Caleb Bingham** to second wife, **Elizabeth "Eliza" Thomas** (December 2)
1850	**Mattie's** residence in 1850 U. S. Census, as a boarder in Lexington, Missouri
1851	Marriage of **Martha Ann "Mattie" Livingston** and **Johnston Lykins**, Lexington, Missouri (October 12)

1851-1852	Honeymoon in Washington, D. C. (October 1851-March 1852)
1852	Arrival of newlyweds **Dr. and Mrs. Johnston Lykins**, and beginning of married life in Westport Landing (aka. Kansas City), Missouri (March)
1853	**Johnston Lykins'** election as first legally elected mayor of Kansas City, Missouri
1854	Passage of **Kansas-Nebraska Act** to open Kansas Indian Territory for Anglo-American settlement
1855	**William Jackson Livingston's** (Mattie Lykins' brother) rental of farm near Hannibal, Missouri
1856	Concealment of **Governor Andrew Reeder** (May)
1856	Destruction of home of **Stephen J. Livingston** (Mattie Lykins' brother) by Free-state/Abolitionist forces (August)
1857	Completion of **Lykins' mansion** on Quality Hill, downtown Kansas City, Missouri (southeast corner of 12th and Washington Streets)
1861	Kansas statehood
1861-1864	Civil War Army Enlistments:
	In the Union Army:
	James Lykins (Joseph Lykins' son) **Claiborne Lykins** (Johnston Lykins' brother)

5

Andrew C. Lykins (Claiborne Lykins' son)
David A. Lykins (Claiborne Lykins' son)
Egbert Freeland Russell
    (Johnston Lykins' son-in-law)
Theodore Case (Johnston Lykins' son-in-law)
George Caleb Bingham
    (Johnston Lykins' close friend)
    Bingham too old to serve in the Army, but he
    enlisted anyway. Mayor Robet T. Van Horn
    used his influence to see to it that Bingham was
    appointed Captain of the Home Guard.
Judson Owen, Assistant Surgeon
    (Mattie Lykins' nephew)

In the Confederate Army:
William J. Livingston (Mattie Lykins' brother)
Spencer McCoy (Johnston Lykins' nephew)

1862-1865	Appointment of **George Caleb Bingham** by **Abraham Lincoln** to serve as Missouri State Treasurer, which office had suddenly been made vacant by the flight of **Governor Claiborne Jackson** and his cabinet to the Confederate States; Bingham lived in Jefferson City
1863	Arrest of **William J. Livingston**, **Mattie Lykins'** brother, for spying (May; executed August 1864)
1863	**Union Prison** collapse, downtown Kansas City, Missouri, which **Mattie** was eye-witness (August 14)
1863	Raid of **Quantrill's** guerrillas on Lawrence, Kansas, to which **Mattie** was eye-witness (August 21)

1863	Issuance of "General Orders No. 11," commonly called "Order No. 11," by **Union General Thomas Ewing** (August 25)
1863	Banishment of **Mattie Lykins** from Kansas City for disloyalty
1864	Arrest of **Claiborne Lykins** near St. Joseph, Missouri (January; he died in 1877)
1864	Return of **Mattie Lykins** to Kansas City (January)
1865-1869	Creation of painting, *"Martial Law,"* by **George Caleb Bingham** while at his home in Independence. Quickly became popularly known as, *"Order No. 11"*
1866	Campaign of Mattie to found **Confederate Widows' and Orphans' Home**, with **Mattie** as President of the Society for the Home (July)
1870	Relocation of **George Caleb Bingham** to Kansas City. His studio was on the third floor of the building on the southwest corner of 3rd and Main Streets in downtown Kansas City. Between 1870 and 1876, Bingham painted a second copy, or version of *"Martial Law,"* or, *"Order No. 11."*
1874	Establishment and construction of (Statewide) **Widows' and Orphans' Home** with **Mattie** as Superintendent, Kansas City, Missouri. (Cornerstone dedicated and laid June 24)
1874	Legislative withdrawal of funds from Statewide **Widows' and Orphans' Home**

1874	Bankruptcy **of Johnston Lykins** after his assets eroded during the martial law years, and as a result of the rampant speculation and ensuing "Panic of 1873"
ca. 1875	Establishment of **The Lykins Institute**, an academy for young women
1876	Sale of the **Lykins mansion** to **John Mastin**
1876	Death of **Johnston Lykins** at The Lykins Institute, Kansas City, Missouri (August 15)
1876	Death of **Elizabeth "Eliza" (Thomas) Bingham**, **George Caleb Bingham**'s second wife (November 3)
1878	Marriage of **Martha Ann "Mattie" (Livingston) Lykins** and **George Caleb Bingham** at The Lykins Institute, Kansas City, Missouri (June 18)
1879	Death of **George Caleb Bingham** at The Lykins Institute, Kansas City, Missouri (July 7)
1882	Sale of Widows' and Orphans' Home property to the **Little Sisters of the Poor**
1889	Moving of the **Lykins mansion by George W. Strope** across the street from the southeast corner to the southwest corner of 12th and Washington Streets
1890	Death of **Martha Ann "Mattie" (Livingston) Lykins Bingham**, Kansas City, Missouri (September 20)
1893	Auction to settle Bingham's estate, including Mattie's portrait, *"Mrs. General Bingham"* (March 25)

CHAPTER 1

Mattie's Southern Roots

Exciting new lives stretched before Mattie Livingston, age 18, and her sister Rebecca as they rode the steamboat up the Mississippi River to Lewis County, Missouri, in 1842. Rebecca was there to marry Thomas J. Hughes, one of many of the Hughes who had come to Missouri to settle in its earliest days. Missouri, the 24th state, was only in its 19th year when the two sisters arrived to begin their adult lives in the state where land-hungry settlers rushed in on the heels of Lewis and Clark's storied exploration.

Mattie and the State of Missouri, born within three years of each other, were formed together in the crucible of the national debate over states' rights and the institution of slavery. The Missouri Compromise, which permitted Missouri to enter the Union as a slave state, was a provision designed to lessen the increasingly bitter sectarian division between the Northern and Southern regions of the country. The bill solved the immediate issue of containing the expansion of slavery into the western territories, but the underlying conflicts remained and deepened in the following decades. In an 1820 letter to John Holmes, Thomas Jefferson wrote:

> *This momentous question [the bill forging the Missouri Compromise], like a fire bell in the night, awakened and filled me with terror. I considered it at once as the knell of the Union. It is hushed indeed for the moment, but this is a reprieve only, not a final sentence. A geographical line, coinciding with a marked principle, moral and political, once conceived and held up to the angry passions of men, will never be obliterated; and every new irritation will mark it deeper and deeper.*

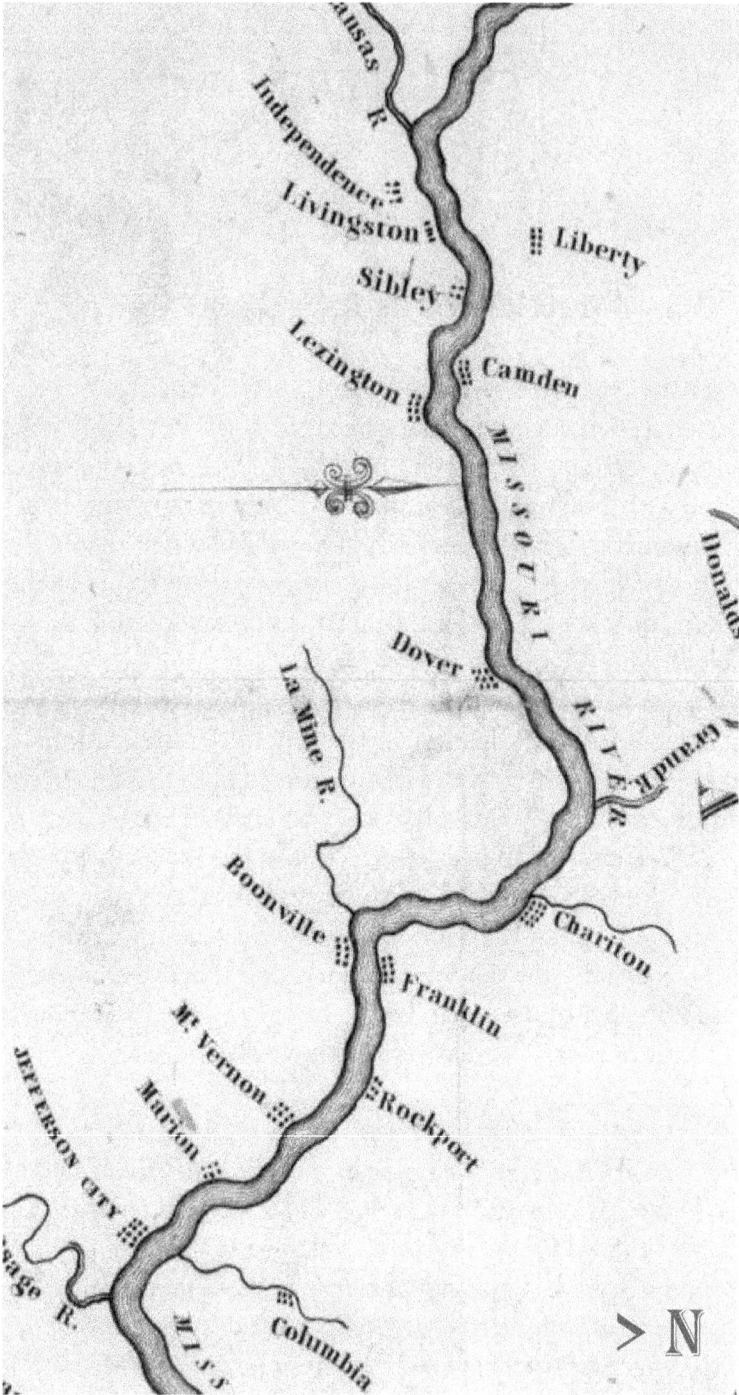

Missouri was destined to become a symbol and crossroad for these regional differences and, as a citizen of the fledgling state, Mattie was to experience firsthand the deadly outcome of the two conflicting visions of America.

For better or for worse, Mattie's new home was Missouri. After twenty-year old Rebecca married,[1] she, her husband and Mattie made their home near Jefferson City, a site chosen as state capitol specifically because of its location. In 1840, the capitol city had a population of 1700 and was expected to become a major city because of its centrality as a way point for steamboats carrying provisions and westward bound settlers up the Missouri toward Westport and Independence, a trail head for the Santa Fe Trail. Rebecca's husband, Thomas, was an enthusiastic entrepreneur, capitalizing on the push westward: he owned an interest in the steamboat "Sacramento" which carried passengers on the Mississippi and Missouri Rivers as far as Kanesville, Iowa.

In addition to its position as a burgeoning trade center and frontier town, Jefferson City would have also provided a great deal of political intrigue and entertainment for his bright, well-educated sister-in-law Mattie. The state's second capitol building was completed shortly before she arrived and dominated the surrounding landscape on a bluff overlooking the Missouri River.

In Mattie's childhood, she was thoroughly immersed in the views of slavery and states' rights which had come to Missouri straight from their cultural origins in Virginia, Maryland and Kentucky. Many of the first settlers of Kentucky (then part of Virginia), including her father, grandparents and great-grandparents, were from the mid-Atlantic states of Virginia and Maryland, and, more distantly, from England, Scotland and Ireland. Mattie's grandfather, Francis Jackson, came to Kentucky from Amelia County, Virginia in 1787 as a veteran of the Revolutionary War and settled near Frankfort; her paternal grandfather was a member of a distinguished Maryland family. As Frankfort and the farms around it developed, gracious brick and white Georgian homes graced the lush green landscape where race horses and bourbon reflected the residents' Scottish roots. The mid-Atlantic settlers transplanted the reliance on slave labor, cultural beliefs and architecture to the spacious blue-grass region where Mattie was born.

Map of central Kentucky showing Mattie's birthplace, near Frankfort and Shelbyville, where she resided on the Owen Plantation before leaving for Missouri.

In central Missouri, seven counties along the Missouri River came to be known as "Little Dixie." Unlike other parts of Missouri, the counties' primary crops—tobacco, hemp, and, later, cotton—demanded a large labor force for their cultivation and harvesting. In 19th century America, that demand translated into the use of slaves on the farms and plantations across the southern tier of the nation and on into Missouri as settlers poured in from Tennessee and Kentucky.

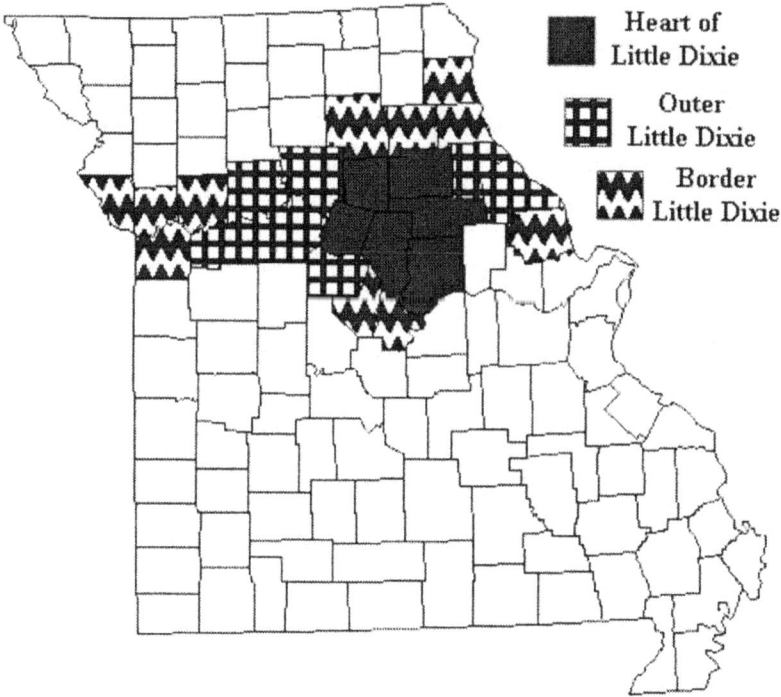

The agricultural practice and culture were similar to those in Kentucky; however, Little Dixie did not have the large plantations that characterized the Deep South where farmers routinely held 20 or more slaves to farm their land. Farmers in central Missouri more typically had 6-8 slaves and other households tended to have one or two domestic servants. Jefferson City was not in one of the seven counties most heavily engaged in the use of slave labor; however, the two counties directly north of it, Callaway and Boone Counties, were deep in the heart of Little Dixie. Still, the Kentucky-based Thomas J. Hughes household likely had one or two domestic servants. Mattie's brother-in-law in Kentucky, in whose house she resided from 1838-1842, was a much more substantial slave-holder, reporting 25 slaves in the 1850 Slave Schedule.

Mattie shuttled between her two sisters' homes, spending periods of time with each. She was close to the children of both families throughout her life: Rebecca's son, Alphonse Hughes, born in 1846 and William and Elizabeth Owen's six children in Shelby County, Kentucky, born between 1838 and 1854. When her sisters needed her assistance, she was there. When she was not attending school or writing serial stories for the newspaper, she cared for children. At the age of seventeen, she published a serialized story, "The Forest Cottage," in *The Shelby News* while living with the Owen family. Her propensity for care-giving, her bright, spirited intellect, and her quick tongue were hallmarks of her life and manifested themselves from her earliest days in Missouri.

Mattie and the Hughes family moved to Middletown (now Waverly), Missouri, a major center for raising hemp, shortly before Thomas died unexpectedly in 1848, leaving a young widow of 27 and young children.[2] Rebecca faced a prolonged battle over her husband's estate, and she and Mattie moved to Lexington where Mattie established a school for girls and lived in a boarding house.

Handwritten excerpt from Martha A. Livingston's scrapbook titled, "The Forest Cottage"

The two sisters were familiar with the necessity of moving forward following the death of a family member. Both their parents had died by the time Mattie was three years old. Mattie, and perhaps some of her five brothers and sisters, lived with her grandmother, Sarah Livingston, in Frankfort, Kentucky, for the next ten years. Mattie began school in Frankfort and completed her education in Shelbyville following the death of her grandmother when Mattie was about twelve. One of Mattie's earliest published romances, "Mary Sharp," features a young girl who is forced out into the world because of her mother's impending death, a plot resonating with Mattie's own experience.

For the next four years, Mattie lived with her sister, Elizabeth, and William Wooten Owen. By the end of the 1840s, most of her brothers and sisters had reached adulthood and half of them had left Kentucky. Her brother, John Henry Livingston, struck out for California during the Gold Rush of 1849 and settled in Contra Costa County across the bay from San Francisco.[3] John Henry

**Martha A. Livingston's
"Mary Sharp," from, *The Shelby News***

may even have ridden on his brother-in-law's steamboat as he made his way west. The Missouri River was a major artery to Independence where the California, Oregon and Santa Fe Trails originated. The primary occupation for settlers living between St.

16

Louis and Independence was transporting and provisioning westward-bound wagon trains. As many other gold rush hopefuls quickly moved out of Contra Costa, to search for gold, John Henry married an Irish immigrant from Canada and settled down to carpentry. He also served as Deputy Coroner of Contra Costa probably because his carpentry business entailed building coffins, a hot commodity in the gold rush days of California.

Elizabeth Owen, and two brothers, Stephen and William, continued to live in Kentucky in the 1840s, while Mattie and Rebecca were Missouri pioneers carrying with them the Kentucky blue-grass attitudes with which they had been raised.

CHAPTER 2

Growing with Kansas City

The 1850s brought a change of direction to the 27-year-old school teacher's life. A widowed father of one of her students in Lexington, Missouri, took notice of the witty, spirited Martha Ann Livingston. In October 1851, Mattie married Johnston Lykins, who was 24 years her senior.

Martha A. "Mattie" (Livingston) Lykins
by S. M. Eby & Son, Ambrotype and Photographic Artists,
Kansas City, Missouri, 1865
Mattie was the first woman to have a photo made in Kansas City
Courtesy Jackson County Historical Society, Gift of Robert D. Owen

Dr. Johnston Lykins
portrait by George Caleb Bingham
Courtesy
Bingham-Waggoner Historical Society
313 West Pacific
Independence, Missouri

After 30 years with the Baptist Mission, Johnston had left his missionary calling partly out of disenchantment with the Baptists' inability to support the missionary work and partly out of the need to care for the three children left behind when his first wife, Delilah (McCoy) Lykins, died. He continued to practice medicine in Westport.

Johnston Lykins was clearly smitten with Mattie, publishing ardent poems in *The Metropolitan*, a local newspaper. In a honeymoon poem, "Lines by a Missionary to his Wife," he wrote from Washington, D.C.:

For the Metropolitan.
Lines by a Missionary to His Wife:

'Tis to thee my thoughts are wending—
Idol of devoted heart—
All its love to thee is tending,
For I know that we must part.

20

'Tis twilight now—the stars are shining
Like gems on azure sea—
But softer, sweeter, is that twining
Which binds my heart to thee.

And the balmy breeze is passing—
Laden with its rich perfume—
But how far, how much surpassing,
Is of love, the budded bloom.

Eve has come; its holy biding
Falls like light upon the soul,
And I feel of faith its chiding
As fears upon me roll.

Living alone, I have been straying
For ____ and battle field,
While martyr peers still are praying,
Holding forth the warriors shield.

Turn I must, and be hasting
From the home I love so well,
Moments fly and hours are wasting,--
Oh! How sad away to dwell.

But from thee, love, I am not flying
From thy bosom never
Where'er I in life or dying
Thy heart's my home forever.

Western Mo. 1851

What he lacked in poetic technique he made up for in affection! In marrying Johnston, Mattie also acquired an extended family. Sarah Lykins, her former student, emulated Mattie, writing poetry and serialized stories and, prior to her marriage, teaching school. Though Sarah had now married, she and Mattie remained close; Johnston's other two children, William H. R. and Juliana, ages 23 and 12 respectively, formed abiding lifelong relationships with her as well. Other members of Johnston's family, five brothers and several nieces and nephews, had come to Missouri and the Kansas Territory and many of them, too, became part of the fabric of her life.

The newlyweds took a honeymoon trip to Washington, D.C., spending the winter there. Mattie wrote her first impressions of the nation's capitol, published in Kansas City's *Metropolitan* in late 1851. The letter, quoted in part, underscores her patriotic fervor and an eerie prescience regarding her country's future:

> *This is my first visit to Washington, and, as a matter of course, I gaze about with as much curiosity as though I were a visitant from a neighboring planet—seeing much to admire and much to condemn. Shortly after my arrival, I found myself wending my way to the capitol; I ascended the mighty dome and here I am at a loss to describe my feelings. The view before me, and the magnificent building upon which I stood, kindled the spark of patriotism into a bright blaze, and I felt proud of my country, proud of her public institutions and her laws, however much abused they may be, and the veneration and respect that I have ever entertained for Washington, and our fathers of the Revolution, rose higher and higher, until I felt, as I believe, woman never felt. But, in the midst of these thoughts and feelings, the sad recollection stole over my mind that the cry of disunion had been heard in the halls beneath me, and I trembled, my very lifestrings quivered as the emotions of pleasure and pain came in contact. I murmured; away, with the man or men*

22

that would sever the golden cord which binds the states of this Union together, as a band of sisters. He who would stab to the heart this family with the dagger of desolation, ruin, misery, and unhappiness is not the offspring of our ancestors, but beings destitute of every shad of high, noble and sterling principle, whose mission is to disseminate the poisonous seed of disunion, strife and discord, which will eventually deluge our happy country in blood; and the widow's moan, and the orphan's wail, will again be echoed from north to south, from east to west.

Returning from their honeymoon to Missouri in the Spring of 1852, Mattie and Johnston began their life together in Kansas City, a small settlement across the river from the Kansas Indian Territory and the gateway to the far west. Mattie recalled in her journal the excitement their steamboat's arrival occasioned:

> *. . . we landed in Kansas City the first week in March 1852. The boat on which we had taken passage at St. Louis, was the second one to reach our wharf that spring. In those days the arrival of the first steamboats of the season was generally hailed with delight and usually brought to the levee, every man and boy in our town.*
>
> *For the three winter months of the year we were locked in from the busy world by ice and snow, hence the opening of navigation was recognized as the key that unlocked the door to commercial life and activity.*

Kansas City was a straggly little town in its infancy in 1852, but Johnston was aware of the potential for a large urban center to develop there because of the town's advantageous location and abundant natural resources.

KANSAS CITY IN 1855.

As early as 1836 Johnston envisioned a large city developing on the great bend of the Missouri River and bought seventeen acres there. Mattie's early impression of the town was not glowing, but, as she wrote about it years later, she looked back on the fledgling village with fond good humor:

> At that time, Kansas City could hardly be called even a village. It was better known as Westport Landing, grouped along the levee were a few cheaply constructed warehouses and two or three stores which consisted of a mixed stock of goods. This meant everything from calico and silk down to groceries, hardware, tinware, ready made clothing and shoes for man and beast. We had one little drug store that dealt chiefly in quinine and patent medicines. In this little ten by fifteen foot room, our worthy postmaster found quarters for himself, and an old goods box with less than a dozen pigeon holes in it for the reception and safe keeping of our once-a-week mail. A shoe mending shop, several saloons and the

24

Gillis House about comprised the entire list of buildings on the levee. . . .

Our town then numbered in population less than three hundred, whites, negroes and Indians all told. Our only official guardian was a township marshal who was rarely to be found when needed. A little log Catholic church presided over by Father Donnelly, was the only place of worship nearer than Westport or Independence.

The tenor of Mattie's writing in her journal is that of an intrepid, engaged woman relishing her life as a pioneer adventuress. Her first year of marriage called on her resilience and resourcefulness as she encountered life on what was then the American Frontier. She recalled an encounter with Indians during her first year at Westport Landing:

In 1852 the Indians roamed our streets in all their native freedom and often without the least fear of disturbance, they slept in the tall weeds and hazel brush that grew on our hills in patches. In the month of December our farmers generally killed their hogs and sold to us our year's meat which we cut up and salted away without ever a thought of such an enemy to human life as [trichinosis]. Usually about hog killing time and during the ripening of the different kinds of wild fruits that grew abundantly with us, the Indians were our most frequent and troublesome visitors. The first year of my housekeeping, I well remember one morning in December, just as I was about to leave my room for the kitchen to superintend the making of our sausage meat and head cheese. I was called hastily to see a neighbor's child, which had at that moment met with a serious accident. On my return home, I found our kitchen in possession of ten or fifteen Indians [sic.] braves with as many squaws and papooses. Not a living soul was to be

25

*seen about the premises, save the loud talking Indians.
Two or three squaws had contentedly seated themselves
before the fire and were cooking pieces of meat tied to the
end of long sticks while their companions were
examining the contents of our kitchen cupboard.
Suddenly they discovered me entering the back porch and
with one bound the whole band rushed towards me
wildly gesticulating and by every sign they could invent
tried to tell me that something had happened which they
wanted to explain. I confess I was badly frightened and
hardly knew whether to stand my ground or to seek
protection at one of our neighbors. However, I mustered
up sufficient courage to stamp my foot quite vigorously
and at the same time I pointed toward the yard gate as a
command for them to leave. They evidently mistook my
meaning and thought I meant to tell them that they had
driven our servants off through the yard gate.
Immediately a big, dirty, tough looking Indian brave
caught me by the arm and more dragging than leading
me, ran towards the stable that stood on the rear part of
the lot. Laughing immoderately, he pointed towards the
upper part of the stable from which I understood that our
servants had taken refuge there. At once, I loudly called
our woman servant by name. She silently responded by
showing her face at a window in the loft. The colored boy
then grew bold and thrust his inky head out at another
opening in the stable. Assuring them there was really no
harm in the Indians, I bade them come down and go
back to their work. With due alacrity and generosity, I
filled their sacks with hog's heads and meat, after which
they left without ceremony. The following winter the
same band returned and I traded them meat and flour
for parched squaw corn and hominy.
      During the summer and fall months we depended
chiefly on the Indians for our fruit and berries for*

preserving. It seemed to afford them pleasure to bring to
our doors, on their ponies, nice baskets of wild
strawberries, blackberries, gooseberries, grapes, plums and
wild crab apples thickly covered over with paw-paw
leaves to protect them from the heat ~~and~~ of the sun.
Among the many other good services they rendered us,
they kept our tables supplied bountifully with the best of
dried buffalo meat and with a kind of parched corn,
which when cooked, was delicious enough for the gods to
eat.

Primitive as the city was in 1852, the couple relished pioneering together and thrived in Westport. With Johnston, Mattie's new life strongly engaged her imagination and abilities: the nurturance of children, her teaching and writing interests, and her skill in community leadership. Johnston, highly regarded as a parent, community leader and visionary intellectual, was a good match for her, and the two quickly became central to the development of the community. While Johnston vigorously supported Westport's growth, he and Mattie nurtured the social and spiritual well-being of the village, too.

GREAT BEND IN THE MISSOURI RIVER AT KANSAS CITY FROM AN OLD PRINT

When the first Methodist church was built, Mattie organized the Westport women into a sewing society to raise funds for heating and lighting the new church. The women decided to hold a fundraising fair in early December, 1852, and Mattie chaired the planning committee. After being suddenly called away to Louisville in October, Mattie left the planning to the group; that, however, proved to be a disaster. The women gridlocked in dissension and did not meet until Mattie's return to Westport in early December. At that point, the severe winter had iced in all the steamboats and it was impossible to get goods to sell at the fair—Mattie, however, had cannily secured items to sell as she made her way northward from Louisville just before the ice closed off Westport.

As she thought about where the fair could be held, she remembered an acquaintance who owned a steamboat stranded in the river's ice at the landing and he graciously gave her permission to use the steamboat as the location of the fair. She and the Westport women then held not one, but two, fundraising events on the boat. *"These two entertainments,"* Mattie wrote, *"netted our society $500. With a population of less than four hundred, I venture to say that no fair held since in our city in proportion to population has ever excelled in its receipts the first fair ever held in Kansas City. To the trustees of the church we turned over the $500 which warmed, lighted and carpeted the first Protestant church ever erected in Kansas City."* (As noted earlier, Mattie referred to both Westport Landing and Kansas City interchangeably when she wrote of her earliest days there.)

A local minister approached Johnston to ask him to become the Methodist Sunday School's superintendent; Johnston declined, but suggested that Mattie might do it. Mattie took up the challenge of transmitting religious instruction to unruly local boys who weren't at all sure they wanted to "get religion." After Mattie had matched wits with them, they became model students!

After the first mayor of Kansas City was found to have been illegally elected because he did not reside in the city, Johnston, as chairman of the City Council, became the first legally elected mayor in 1853. His contributions to the city in ensuing years included the

28

establishment of a newspaper, assuming the Presidency of the Mechanics Bank, and convening a railroad committee to bring the railroad to Kansas City rather than to Leavenworth. He tirelessly promoted immigration to the region, corresponding with numerous Eastern and Southern newspapers about the area's promise. In 1855-56, Johnston wrote a series of letters in the city newspaper, *The Enterprise*, which was designed to build public support for Kansas City as a railroad and commercial center. "Commerce," wrote Lykins, "like the star of empire wends its way to the West; and commerce creates at given distances commercial centres." Lykins suggested the awe-inspiring consequences of completing these projects. The tropical South and the temperate North, the agricultural fertility of the West, and the industrial power of the East–all would meet in this great central emporium. Nature had made it potentially the hub of direct trade with an area which stretched away over a thousand miles in every direction.

Increasingly, Johnston's attention was drawn to the economic development of the region, while Mattie wrote serialized novelettes for her newspaper audiences in Lexington, Missouri, and Kansas City. She had an avid following of readers, as noted by one of the editors.

Throughout the 1850s, she wrote romantic tales of sisters separated by

"The Twin Sisters; or, The Scattered Household,"

The above is the title of an original story, the publication of which we shall commence in our next paper. It was written expressly for the *Western Metropolitan*, by one of the most talented ladies in this section of the country, is well conceived, the characters beautifully delineated, the whole tenor a moral, and in all it will prove a most interesting romance. It will be continued through a number of papers, and those desirous of reveling in the enjoyment of an intellectual feast, should commence with its first appearance in the *Metropolitan* of next week, carefully preserving each succeeding number until the completion of the story by our fair and gifted authoress.

circumstance, of orphaned, abandoned young ladies, of gallant men coming to the rescue, and of twists and turns in their stories caused by lucky accident. Her writing was well within the genre of the serialized romantic novel which enjoyed great popularity from 1820-1860.

☞ THE STORY.—The "Two Orphans," will occupy our columns for some weeks to come, and we feel a just pride in saying that it is equal in all respects to the much puffed and lauded prize tales of the Magazines.— This is the second story from the same pen, and we sincerely hope it will not be the last. The conception and plot are excellent, and the style and execution worthy of authors of much greater pretensions. We feel, gratefully, the compliment extended our paper by being the medium of its introduction to the reading public, but for the sake of the authoress, could have wished a more extended literary medium for its presentation. We know we but echo the wish of our readers that this will not be the last feast to which they shall be invited.

"The Twin Sisters; or, The Scattered Household,"
The above is the title of an original story, the publication of which we shall commence in our next paper. It was written expressly for the *Western Metropolitan*, by one of the most talented ladies in this section of the country; is well conceived, the characters beautifully delineated, the whole tenor a moral, and in all it will prove a most interesting romance. It will be continued through a number of papers, and those desirous of reveling in the enjoyment of an intellectual feast, should commence with its first appearance in the *Metropolitan* of next week, carefully preserving each succeeding number until the completion of the story by our fair and gifted authoress.

The couple was happy and successful during this period of their lives, even as the likelihood of Civil War increased. From the time the Kansas-Nebraska Act passed in 1854, regional differences, the question of slavery, and the lust for land engulfed the daily occupations on both sides of the Missouri-Kansas Territory border. Early Missouri settlers from Kentucky and Tennessee were determined to make the Kansas Territory, opened in 1855 to white settlers, a slave state. Settlers pouring in from the north and east were equally determined to create Kansas as a free state. Prior to this time, the westward migration of northern and southern settlers had moved in parallel and largely separate paths across the continent. Now the two forces were to meet headlong on the plains of Kansas. Three of Mattie's five brothers and sisters had settled in Missouri or the Kansas Territory. Her brother William Jackson Livingston settled in Eastern Missouri near Palmyra, a town sometimes called, "the Charleston of the West."[4] It was a stronghold of Southerners and William soon affiliated himself with them.

Her brother, Stephen J. Livingston, on the other hand, settled in the Kansas Territory alongside Mattie's stepson, W. H. R. Lykins, in 1855. Finding himself surrounded by the abolitionists who settled Lawrence, Stephen chose the course of staunch neutrality, but that did not save him from being held under arrest for two days by proslavery forces or from having Jayhawkers destroy his home. Having served briefly as justice of the peace in Lawrence, both sides distrusted him.[5] To get out of the line of fire, he and his family moved to a farm further from Lawrence.

Young W. H. R. Lykins, a "sovereign squatter," had posted his claim on the first possible day the territory opened. In a land dispute with Massachusetts' Emigrant Aid Society, the disputed claim was divided and W. H. R., along with the Emigrant Aid Society, became the founders of Lawrence, Kansas. Four of Johnston's brothers all made land claims in the Kansas Territory when it opened to white settlement. Even Johnston joined in the fray, claiming that even though he was a Missourian he had a right to vote in the upcoming territorial elections. W. H. R. stockpiled supplies in his cabin in preparation for the hundreds of Missourians who streamed across the border to vote for candidates running for election to the first Kansas legislature.

Historian Theodore Brown identified 31 of 39 Kansas City leaders in the 1850s as having come to Missouri from south of the Ohio River and many were slave owners. Culturally and by family relationship, their sympathies leaned toward the south, but economically they were oriented toward westward growth and expansion. These two conflicting interests dominated the actions of many Kansas City leaders during the Border War.

Though he was inclined toward the Southern point of view, Mattie's husband argued for peace and reason from the beginning of the conflict. He and other businessmen of Kansas City launched a series of town meetings urging citizens to protect property, keep trade flowing through the city, and maintain order. Their overriding

31

concern was that the fledgling city not be eclipsed by nearby urban rivals, Leavenworth, Kansas and St. Joseph, Missouri.

A letter from "Cato" in Mattie's scrapbook, probably written by Johnston Lykins, urged established residents of Kansas City to treat newcomers fairly:

Communicated
For the *Enterprise*

Ms. Editor,

Within the past week quite a number of eastern emigrants have landed at our city, bound for the territory lying West of our state. Among them we have noticed many of apparently great intelligence, and business tact. Seeking a home in the beautiful territory of Kansas, they come to erect Mills, and to establish other machinery calculated to greatly facilitate the development of the country; and in their deportment we have recognized nothing exceptionable, but to the contrary, much to commend.

The arrival of these emmigrants has been looked upon with much interest by the citizens of Upper Missouri, and, in some places, unkind and inflammatory speeches have been made calculated to sour in advance the public mind against them. This it seems to me is wrong. If our laws should be violated, the remedy is plain, but good and law abiding citizens should not be prejudged....

The right then which pertains to Georgia should pertain to Massachusetts also, and this appears to be the only reasonable view to be taken of the subject. The evil lies in interfering with the rights of others, and not in the coming of orderly peaceable, intelligent and worthy men, loving their institutions and customs as we love ours. Without conceding an iota of our own strong southern

feelings which we in infancy imbibed in the sunny South,
we admit their right to come and bid them welcome as
passengers to their new home. Let the ballot box be the
umpire.

CATO

As the Border War raged around them, Mattie and Johnston were caught up in the events. Proslavery advocates were infuriated with Territorial Governor Andrew Reeder, believing that he had betrayed them and their cause when he was appalled by the Missourians' fraudulent takeover of the Kansas Territorial election and supported overturning the elections in disputed districts. A grand jury of the proslavery First Kansas Territorial Legislature indicted Reeder for treason and sought to have him removed from office. President Pierce forced Reeder's resignation, but for a different reason. Reeder had engaged in shady, self-serving real estate speculation related to the establishment of the State Capitol. The proslavery forces were not satisfied—they preferred to hang him.

Three men in Westport formed a plan to help Reeder escape from the Missouri-Kansas borderland; one of the three was Johnston Lykins. In her journal, Mattie described the May 1856 escapade:

Well do I remember the night of his flight to Kansas City and his place of concealment here for several weeks. A number of young, hot-headed southerners had organized themselves into a military company for the purpose of preventing settlers from entering Kansas. This self organized and indiscreet company determined to intercept Governor Reeder and capture him if possible. They had very rightly supposed that he would make his way to Kansas City through some secret channel and from this point would make his escape by boat to St. Louis. In order to cut off his retreat and to effect his capture they stationed pickets on the levee and searched every boat that landed at our wharf from the Upper Missouri. Col[onel] Coates [Kersey], Dr. Lykins and Mr. Eldridge of the Eldridge House, afterwards known as the

Gillis [sic.] *Hotel, were the only gentlemen in our city who were informed in reference to his movements. They had purposely delayed his coming to Kansas City as long as they could with the hope that the excitement then existing might abate.*

OLD GILLIS HOUSE

Gilliss House is the proper spelling of this great, western hotel on the Missouri River, at one time known—among a variety of names—as the Eldridge Hotel, which Mattie mentioned in her "Recollections of Old Times in Kansas City."

However, he was so hotly pressed by his enemies in the rear that his friends finally decided that it would not be safe to longer postpone his escape from Kansas. Hence, it was arranged that on a certain night a skiff should be sent up the river by a trusty man to a designated point where Gov[ernor] Reeder would be in waiting. In the meantime, the men who had been standing guard for so many long hot days and nights had really relaxed in vigilance and greatly reduced the number of pickets. Fortunately the night Gov[ernor] Reeder was expected, there was but one picket on duty. The remainder of the company had retired for the night to a room used as headquarters in a building on the corner of Main Street and the Levee.

Between one and two o'clock that night, under the shelter of a starless sky, this lone picket was startled by the dipping of oars and the splashing of water. Looking in the direction from whence the sound came, he discovered a skiff near the shore with two men on it. With one strong stroke of the oarsman, the boat touched the shore. The large[r] man of the two, sprang out and walked rapidly towards the hotel, the door in the basement swung open and he entered without a word being spoken, or the fall of a footstep being heard. The man left the skiff without heeding the command of the picket to halt, struck out in the middle of the stream and was soon lost to sight. The picket was sorely puzzled to account for the maneuvers of the men. After a moment's reflection it occurred to him that the man who had left the skiff and entered the hotel so quietly might possibly be Gov[ernor] Reeder. He hastened to headquarters and imparted his suspicions to his comrades. He urged them to go with him and guard the hotel until morning when they could search the house for the stranger. But the men were too drunk and heavy with stupor to heed his entreaties. They declared they knew the men in the skiff to be negro chicken thieves who had been out on a marauding expedition. Thoroughly disgusted with his comrades in arms, the picket seated himself on a goods box near the door of

35

headquarters and there rested until the sun had risen some distance above the horizon the next morning.

This lone picket was none other than Mr. Alexander Lawton of Georgia after whom Lawton's Addition in this city is named. He was a cultured and refined gentleman but an ardent southerner in sympathy and politics. Feeling the need of a good hot cup of coffee after his night of picket duty, he rang our front door bell just as we had seated ourselves at the breakfast table. He was kindly invited out to the breakfast room and while enjoying his cup of coffee, he related what had taken place on the levee during the night. He further expressed it as his belief that the man who had entered the house was none other than Gov[ernor] Reeder and so strong were his convictions of this, he said he meant to have the hotel searched from cellar to garret during the day. As we knew it had been planned for Gov[ernor] Reeder to come to our city that night by skiff, we felt quite sure that Mr. Lawton was not mistaken in his surmises. Dr. Lykins manifested no particular concern about the story while Mr. Lawton was relating it but hurriedly eating his breakfast asked to be excused giving as a reason that he had several very sick patients to see. He was not long in reaching the Eldridge House and in imparting to Col[onel] Coates and Mr. Eldridge the information he had gained from Mr. Lawton. At once, they took steps to remove Gov[ernor] Reeder to a place of safety. True to his word in the afternoon of the same day, Mr. Lawton had the Eldridge House searched from cellar to garret, but the bird was not in the cage. The place of concealment selected for Gov. Reeder was in the loft of an old house which stood on a hill west of Broadway. It was perfectly obscured by thick hazel brush, paw-paw trees and wild grape vines. During his confinement I often sent him nice things to eat and conveyed to him weekly, clean handkerchiefs and changes of underwear. The torture of suspense and the want of outdoor exercise affected his health and he was soon confined to his cot by nervous prostration and fever.

When it was absolutely necessary for Dr. Lykins to visit him professionally, in order to elude suspicion he would have the wife of the old man who lived in the house to feign sickness and send for hm. As his ill health was really caused by anxiety and close confinement he daily grew weaker and more impatient to be free. His friends realizing that his life depended on his release from confinement planned for his escape on a boat as a wood chopper. . . .

That same year, John Brown and his followers made an incursion into Kansas City, stealing slaves and burning nearby plantations, and many heavily armed strangers bound for the Kansas Territory walked the city streets. Residents who had previously left their doors unlocked now locked them and buried their silver, china and other valuables deep beneath the ground.

Despite the hardships and Borderland conflicts, Mattie thoroughly enjoyed the earliest days of the city. As she looked back at the early 1850s, Mattie recalled:

We had no newspapers, school houses, telegraph lines, market hours, butcher's shops, bakeries, milliner's shop or dressmaking establishments to worry our brains or to drain our pocketbooks.

The latest fashions in dress, parties, luncheons, receptions, operas and the modern club houses with their luxurious trappings did not in the least disturb the quiet of our homes. We lived in blissful ignorance of such pleasures, yet, strange to say, we were a happy and contented people. We wore our ginghams, lawns and calicoes to our best entertainments and a pretty shaker or white corded sunbonnet was the pride of our life. True, we had better gowns and bonnets but they were worn only on rare occasions.

In her "Debby Doolittle" columns Mattie sometimes touched on dissonance between the original Southern and the newer Northern and Eastern settlers of the city. In her journalistic columns for Kentucky newspapers, she assumed the persona of "Debby Doolittle of Hardtack and Pea Ridge" writing to her sister "Jamima in Kaintuck." As Debby Doolittle, she wrote to her sister regarding the new formality that came to the city as it developed. She noted the curious habits of newcomer Yankee women in Kansas City who were bringing with them strange practices such as leaving calling cards and staying at funeral visitations for no more than "2½ minutes." In the guise of Debby, an ignorant, naïve backwoods girl, Mattie commented on contemporary state and local issues, poking fun at

Mattie wrote under the guise or pen name of "Debby Doolittle of Hardtack and Pea Ridge," writing to her sister, "Jamima in Kaintuck."

the ineptitude and laziness of Missouri legislators, depicting them as so fuzzy-headed that they couldn't even find their way to Jefferson City. She often singled out the city "dads;" in one column Debby offered the opinion that the grading of the bluffs to widen and create

steep roads down to the river was actually a device to prevent women from getting together to gossip.

In that time, men involved in real estate development (who were often city councilmen as well) had decided to gouge out streets to traverse from the river bank to the bluffs high above. They moved the limestone from one place to another, filling ravines in some cases and leveling the bluffs. As a result, the roads they created up the newly graded hillsides became the basis for boulevards in today's city and connected the industrial, commercial riverfront to the elite additions above.

"Gully town" created while removal of bluffs 'lowered' streets in Kansas City. On the right was Watkins Bank.
On the left was Mechanics Bank, of which
Johnston Lykins was President.

39

In her journal, written many years later, Mattie wrote more nostalgically of her life as she lived it in the 1850s.

> *. . . our society was not as much mixed then as now. True the circle of our best society was not so extensive but as far as it went, it would be hard to find in our city today, a more intelligent, refined and cultured class of ladies. More than this, they found time to be practical and without the aid of our modern conveniences. In their homes were models of neatness and good order. Their children were never neglected but at all times they were well dressed and well behaved. And be it said to their credit that every stitch in their well made garments was put in by the fingers of their patient and devoted mothers. Not a sewing machine had then crossed the Mississippi river and not a woman lived in our town that had to earn her bread by the needle. No village gossip, no tales or scandal, no divorce suits and no church or neighborhood quarrels ever disturbed the quiet of our social and domestic life. Neither was any woman of an unsavory reputation or one suspected of being unfaithful to her marriage vows ever permitted to enter the "charmed circle of our best society." Money, fine clothes, fine equipages and servants in livery had no value when compared to virtue and gentle breeding and a character above reproach. The refined, pure and primitive simplicity that adorned the domestic and social life of our ladies in those days would reflect no discredit on the ladies of the present age, but would rather tend to throw around their homes a halo of happiness and contentment unknown to many elegant homes and families at the present time.*

As the community's population diversified and grew, the Lykins were at the center of the heady optimism over the young city's potential. By the end of the decade, the population of Kansas

City had burgeoned from 478 and an assessed valuation of taxable property of $54,000 in 1855 to a population of 4,4118 with an assessed valuation of taxable property of $3,311,730 in 1859. Many of the foundations for Kansas City's future growth and prosperity had been laid. Still, the sanguine mood among the city's founding fathers and mothers had tinges of foreboding at its edges. The original settlers from Virginia, Kentucky, and Tennessee now lived cheek to jowl with newer settlers from New York, Pennsylvania and Ohio. All up and down the Borderland of Kansas and Missouri, the countryside was increasingly dangerous and partisan; murder, robbery and para-military actions from both bushwhackers and jayhawkers spilled over.

With the Kansas Territory now attracting thousands of settlers—abolitionists, Free-state farmers and businessmen, and proslavery Southerners-- Kansas City grew rapidly. Throughout the 1850s, businessmen moved to Kansas City to invest in the opportunities they saw for Kansas City to develop into a major metropolitan area and trade center. They established banks, hotels and businesses. They platted new additions and invested in steamboats and rail. The location of the city, at the confluence of the

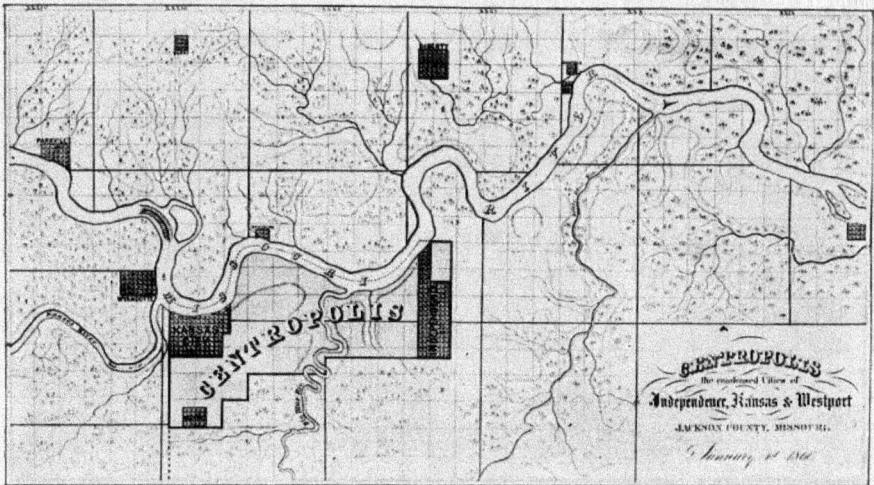

WILLIAM GILPIN'S PROPHETIC MAP, 1859.

41

Missouri and Kansas Rivers, promised to provide a major transportation hub for goods passing across the continent and linking East to West and South to North. Three important wagon trails heading westward originated in Jackson County, Missouri: the Oregon Trail, the Santa Fe Trail, and the California Trail. A visitor to Kansas City, William Gilpin, plotted a map of the area and dubbed it "Centropolis" to signify its destiny to become the place at the center of the continent where all goods, people, and services could join.

One of the early additions established in Kansas City was Quality Hill, a toney suburb on a 200-foot bluff overlooking the industrial West Bottoms and the Missouri River to the North. The Lykins' friend and business associate, Kersey Coates, created the addition a half mile from the West Bottoms and extending from 7th Street on the North to 14th Street on the South. From East to West, it extended from today's I-35 to Broadway.

The brick homes in this addition were sequestered at the ends of shady drives and overlooked the confluence of the Kaw and Missouri Rivers below. There Mattie and Johnston built a sumptuous mansion, hailed as the "finest west of the Mississippi" in 1857. A Director of the Johnson County Kansas Archives, Gerald Motsinger, described the Lykins house on Quality Hill:

> The home, designed in the classic revival style and strongly reminiscent of a Southern mansion, belonged to Dr. and Mrs. Johnston Lykins. Finished in 1857, it became the focal point of the community because both the building and its inhabitants provided a display of reassuring good taste not customarily found on the local scene.
>
> Construction presented many obstacles. A lack of skilled craftsmen forced Lykins to look elsewhere for his builder, and he ultimately hired the Alexander Brothers of Cincinnati. In addition, most of the specialized building materials had to be shipped from

the East. . . . The unusual building duo, one an architect and the other a carpenter, succeeded in creating what many claimed was the "Handsomest mansion west of St. Louis."

The exterior boasted such refinements as intricately detailed shutters and columned porches on front and side, thus providing inviting embellishments to the brick finish. The interior, with its 14 rooms [8 of them were 20-feet-square], 10 fireplaces, wide staircases and crystal chandeliers equaled the best to be found in eastern cities. Located in a community often depicted as consisting of gullies and shanties, it sparkled like a jewel.

Laura Coates Reed, daughter of Mattie Lykins' close friend, Sarah Coates, recalled with pleasure the many hours she spent in the halls of the Lykins mansion, delighting in the profanity of the household parrot, Florita, and seeking the attention of her favorites among the Lykins' servants.

By 1858, Johnston had platted 80 lots in the Lykins Addition. He let it be known that he was not willing to sell to speculators, but to serious builders, and he built a large warehouse there to anchor business development. Within a year, he was president of the powerful Mechanics Bank originating from St. Louis, and he and Mattie had become a very wealthy, powerful couple, deeply committed to the development of the city.

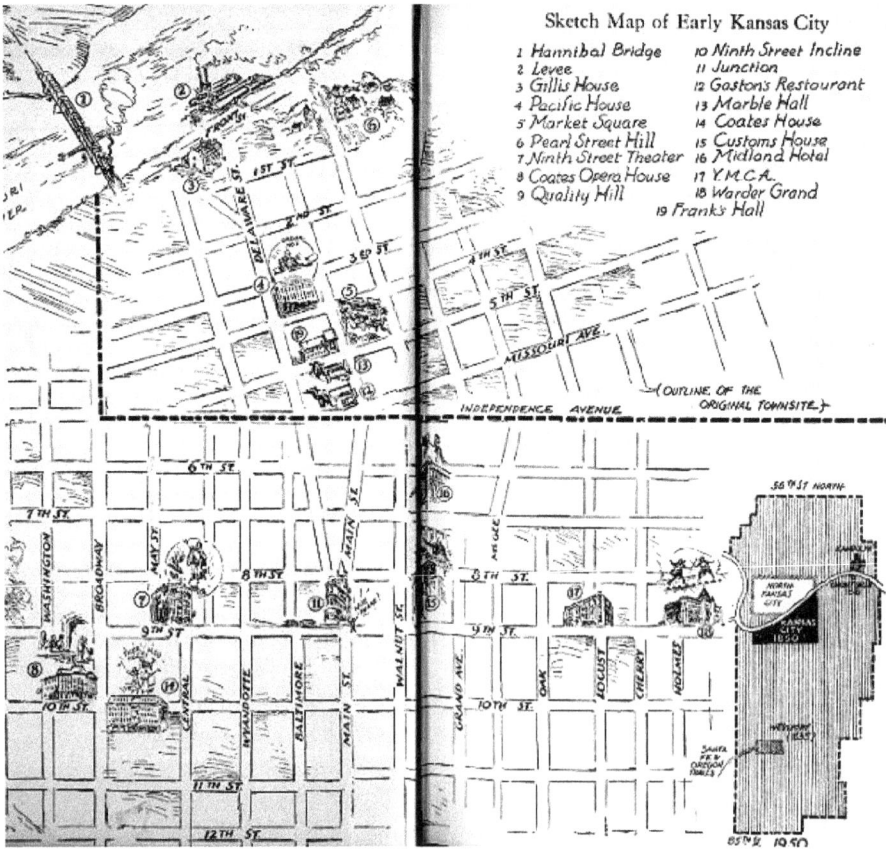

Sketch Map of Early Kansas City

1 Hannibal Bridge
2 Levee
3 Gillis House
4 Pacific House
5 Market Square
6 Pearl Street Hill
7 Ninth Street Theater
8 Coates Opera House
9 Quality Hill
10 Ninth Street Incline
11 Junction
12 Gaston's Restaurant
13 Marble Hall
14 Coates House
15 Customs House
16 Midland Hotel
17 Y.M.C.A.
18 Warder Grand
19 Frank's Hall

CHAPTER 3

Blood and Tears: The Civil War

When the U.S. Census taker came to call on Mattie and
Johnston Lykins in 1860, he found a prosperous family living in a
beautiful mansion on Quality Hill. The value of Johnston's assets,
$60,000, was comparable to 2003's $1,380,000. The couple could
look with pride at what they had accomplished and with hope for
what lay ahead.

Mattie's popularity as a writer and community leader
continued. As president of the Mechanics Bank, Johnston was in the
inner circle of "city dads" building a center of trade and commerce
where steep, muddy paths and log cabins had stretched along the
conjoined rivers less than a decade earlier.

Their home was full of life. Two sons of Mattie's sisters
shared the mansion with them and attended school. Judson Owen, a
22-year-old medical student, and Alphonse Hughes, age 16.

Mattie and Johnston entertained frequently, taking delight in
the dancing of the young people attending their parties. Interesting,
significant conversations with city and state leaders invigorated their
energies and minds: Senator Thomas Hart Benton, General
Stonewall Jackson, painter George Caleb Bingham, attorney and real
estate developer Kersey Coates and his wife, educated, independent-
thinking Sarah Chandler Coates, Theodore Case, newspaper editor
Robert Van Horn and others.

Stimulating as their conversations might have been, the
guests likely avoided discussing some of the pressing issues of the
day: the presidential debates, slavery, and the culture clashes
inherent in the coming of new power players from the East to the
southern-based city. One of the city's most vibrant economic

leaders, Kersey Coates, came to Kansas City from Pennsylvania. He and his wife, Sarah (Chandler) Coates, were Quakers, advocates for the abolition of slavery and proponents of Kansas as a Free State. Regardless of the Coates'political views, the business leaders respected the expertise and powerful economic connections Coates and other newcomers brought to the city.

Theodore Case, husband of Mattie's step-daughter Juliana, noted that while Kansas City residents were predominantly Southern in sympathy, they were actually more interested in making money from both sides than in political issues. They wanted the railroad; they wanted to prevail in their competition with Leavenworth and St. Joseph.

Daniel Geary, one of Mattie's contemporaries, and others who knew Mattie, wrote in their recollections of her that she was "outspoken," and "a rabid Southern sympathizer." It is highly possible that she was not as circumspect in social settings as her determinedly business-oriented husband would have liked. The city fathers had worked very hard to keep a lid on inflammatory language and, no doubt, could see that the national tension over slavery and regional issues had only increased in past years even though warfare along the border had subsided somewhat. Without looking at the situation of Missourians, and more specifically, the residents of Kansas City during the Civil War, it is impossible to fully understand what shaped Mattie's actions and statements during those years.

The issues about to explode into Civil War across the nation were laying barely beneath the surface, unresolved, in Kansas City in 1860.

In the U.S. Slave Schedules of 1860, Johnston's only slaves were a young woman and two young children. Two other slaves, perhaps more able to flee, were listed as having run away. The page on which Johnston's name appeared as slaveholder contains the names of his nearest neighbors. On this page, thirty-one slaves are counted as present and seventeen are listed as having been stolen or having escaped. Kansan abolitionists and jayhawkers' success in freeing Missouri slaves caused the Kansas City skiffs tied at river's edge to be removed and shattered any illusions the slaveholders may have clung to that their slaves were happy to be slaves.

When Abraham Lincoln was elected in 1860, he vowed to halt the expansion of slavery, and that triggered the secession of eleven states of the Union. By the end of April, the newly formed Confederate States of America was at war with those states that had remained in the Union. Governor Claiborne Jackson counted on legislators to vote for Missouri's secession, but Missouri citizens instead sent anti-secessionists to Jefferson City that year.

The situation left the citizens of Missouri in turmoil and confusion, deeply divided in their loyalties. In Kansas City, adherents of both secessionist and anti-secessionists began to demonstrate their loyalties. Mattie's stepson, Theodore Case, described the situation as it was at the beginning of the war:

Early in April, 1861, party spirit ran high, and the adherents of both parties began to hold meetings and to raise their respective flags. The Union party having raised an American flag on the public square, the secessionists determined to offset it with one of their kind. To celebrate the occasion they invited their friends and sympathizers from the surrounding country. Independence, Westport and Clay County responded liberally, and on April 30, the day set for the occasion, a large procession marched through the streets, following a "rebel" flag, and bands playing "rebel" airs, while at the same time numerous Southern flags were displayed from private residences and business houses. The procession moved to the top of a hill at the northeast corner of Second and Main streets, and on this conspicuous position raised their flags to the sounds of martial music and firing of guns. Inflammatory speeches were made which were loudly applauded. Meetings were held and resolutions passed denouncing the government for its efforts to "coerce" the Southern States to remain in the Union, and warning the officials appointed by President Lincoln, not to thrust themselves upon a people who did not want them.

The residents of Kansas City felt the division keenly: because of the city's strategic location, it was in the eye of the storm. Kansas City leaders looked to the west and saw fiercely Unionist Kansas; they looked to the north and saw staunchly Unionist Iowa. To the east was Unionist Illinois. Surrounded by strong Unionist states on three sides, the Southern-leaning population paused. Missouri stuck up like a thumb in the midst of the three states waiting to be smashed if the state seceded. In addition, the business center the Kansas City elite had labored together to build was doomed if the state entered the war.

One of those southern-leaning leaders was Johnston Lykins. He worked with Robert Van Horn, editor of the *Western Journal of Commerce,* to argue passionately against secession. Johnston took a pragmatic approach, writing an open letter to Missourians describing in graphic terms what secession would mean to the state. Although Johnston was "Southern by birth and sympathy" and his wife vociferously favored the Confederacy, Lykins had devoted twenty years of his life to the growth of Kansas City and wrote passionately for the preservation of the Union. Theodore Brown described Johnston Lykins' appeal:

War meant not only the destruction of the beautiful American idea, as Lykins painted it, of a land "where under his own vine and fig trees, the citizen may enjoy the fruits of his labor, with none to molest him or make him afraid. . . ."

War would also bring anarchy and pillage "and subject us to the rule of the tyrant, the robber, the pirate–and our wives, daughters, and mothers to the brutality and lust of fiends in human shape. *Do not say this cannot be–that this is far off–that we shall not see it . . .* " Lykins spared his readers nothing: towns would be sacked, cities destroyed, farms burned, banks robbed. Already, he computed conservatively, the very threat of secession had cost Missourians about $100,000,000 in the decline of property values. Calling attention to his status as an old citizen, Lykins concluded with a strong pro-Union appeal.

In the Spring of 1861, Robert Van Horn defeated a Secessionist candidate for the office of mayor. That winter the Missouri legislature created a strong metropolitan police force for Kansas City which had far-reaching powers and acted independently of the mayor. This police force was Secessionist in its orientation, and gave no assistance to Van Horn in his efforts to maintain law and order in the city. Van Horn wrote that the wealthy seemed to be either secessionist or paralyzed in disbelief. His supporters were German and Irish immigrants and Northerners who had come to live in Kansas City.

Seeing that Kansas City would implode from within, Van Horn rushed to St. Louis to meet with Union General Lyon. As part of his negotiation to gain military protection for Kansas City, Van Horn joined the Union Army and returned to Kansas City as a colonel in that army. He was forced into choosing what he saw as the lesser of evils for the city: martial law and military occupation.

FORT UNION, 1861

The Union positioned three companies in Kansas City and built a small fort at Tenth and Central Streets. The soldiers drilled right under the noses of citizens, and whenever there were frequent military alarms, a huge cannon was fired to rally Unionists to go to the breastworks to protect the fort. The soldiers maneuvered on the hills to the east and west of Broadway, just south of Twelfth Street. In her home at Twelfth and Washington, Mattie was daily witness to the military comings and goings; the war was omnipresent. Kersey and Sarah Coates' daughter wrote:

> *Every event of this stormy period was of gruesome coloring. The cannon was constantly repeating the signal of alarm given by the pickets stationed on the outskirts of the city . . . . Indiscriminate shooting continued among the guards, a bullet whizzing through our bedroom one morning at the break of day. Evidence of war was on every side.*
>
> *Women and children spent many nights in their basements listening to the gunshots in the dark while the men of the house were away on patrol duty.*

Meanwhile, a military government was imposed on the state and Governor Jackson and other state officials left Jefferson City to avoid imprisonment or death. The military command then set up a provisional government complete with another governor. Jackson reconvened his legislative bodies in Neosho, Missouri, and a secession bill was again brought before them. This time, the act of secession proposal passed. The Confederate States of America accepted delegates to their legislature from Missouri, the twelfth state to secede from the Union. Missourians now had two legislatures and two governors, with one of the governments in exile.

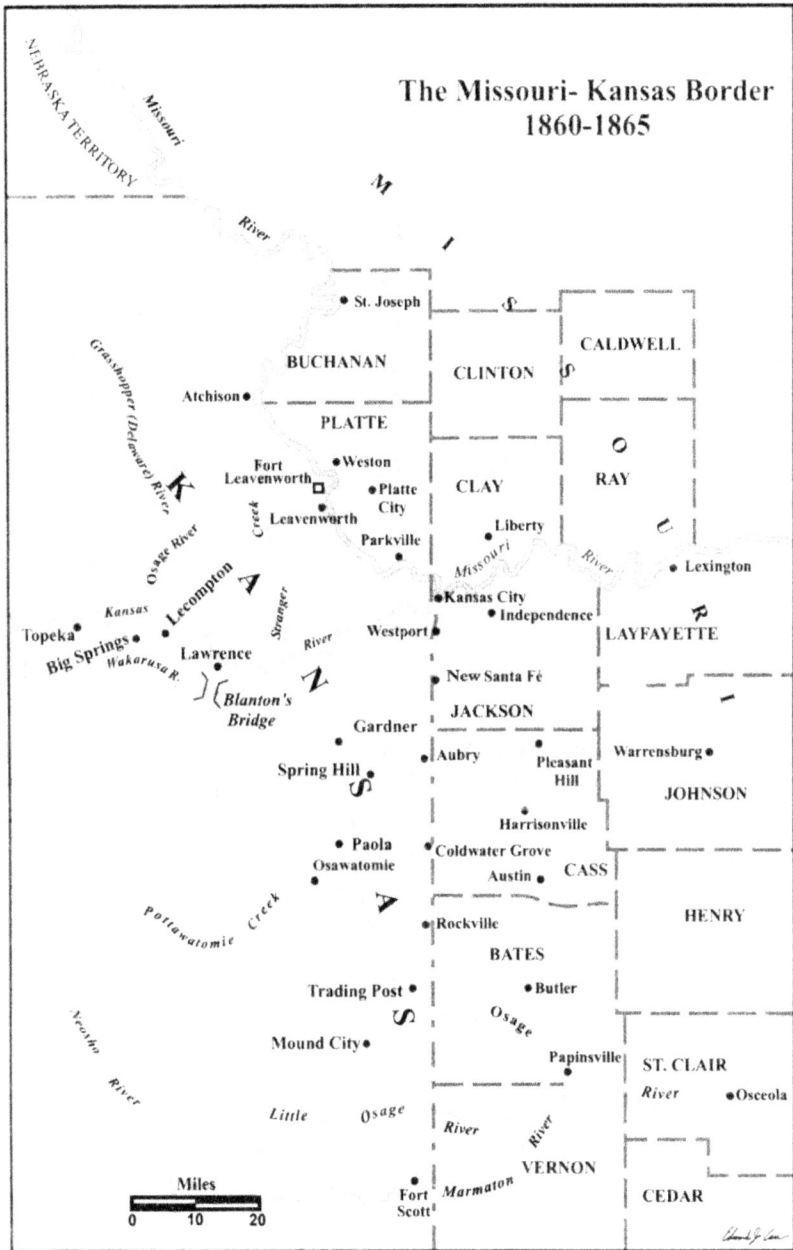

The Missouri- Kansas Border
1860-1865

NEBRASKA TERRITORY

Missouri

River

M
I
S
S
O
U
R
I

St. Joseph

BUCHANAN

CLINTON

CALDWELL

Atchison

PLATTE

RAY

Grasshopper (Delaware) River

Fort Leavenworth
Weston

Platte City

CLAY

Leavenworth

Osage River

Parkville

Liberty

Lexington

Creek

Kansas City

Missouri River

Lecompton

Kansas

Stranger

River

Independence

LAYFAYETTE

Topeka

Big Springs

Wakarusa R.

Lawrence

Westport

New Santa Fé

Blanton's Bridge

JACKSON

Gardner

Aubry

Warrensburg

Spring Hill

Pleasant Hill

JOHNSON

Paola

Coldwater Grove

Osawatomie

Harrisonville

Austin

CASS

Pottawatomie Creek

Rockville

HENRY

BATES

Trading Post

Butler

Neosho River

Mound City

Osage

Papinsville

ST. CLAIR

River

Osceola

Little

Osage

River

River

VERNON

Miles

Fort Scott

Marmaton

CEDAR

0   10   20

51

Historians have never resolved whether the exiled Missouri legislature's vote to secede was legitimate. The House of Representatives' official record of the proceedings was lost during the war, so it is impossible to determine whether there was a quorum for the secession vote or whether a few zealous legislators met without a quorum and voted for secession. Newspapers of the time and the Missouri Senate's records, recovered decades after the war, indicate that there was a quorum and that the vote was legitimate. Jackson's government relocated in Arkansas to wait for their military leader, General Sterling Price, to restore them to their place in Missouri. The provisional government, supported by Union forces, remained in Jefferson City and, from the perspective of Unionists, the State of Missouri had never, and would never, leave the Union.

At this juncture, old assumptions about where Mattie's associates might stand came under intense self-examination. Mattie and fellow residents of Kansas City had to decide what to do: (1) cooperate with or submit to the Unionists now predominating in Kansas City; (2) engage in acts of resistance; (3) leave their properties in Kansas City and go elsewhere. Lyon raised three regiments of soldiers in St. Louis to be stationed in Kansas City. The following discussion and chart encapsulate the directions that some of Mattie's closest circle of friends and associates took.

Mattie's Circle of Loyalties Outside Kansas City

Two of **Johnston's brothers** aligned themselves with the Confederacy, each operating independently in the borderland towns they lived it. **Claiborne**, a founding pioneer in St. Joseph, was arrested for engaging in subversive activities—stealing horses destined, presumably, for Confederate guerrilla fighters. After recovering from a wound he received during his midnight thievery, he was released from prison on bail and fled to his sister in Iowa while he waited and hoped for an acquittal. Johnston's brother **David**

Lykins, a resident of Paola, Kansas, was an outspoken proponent of the proslavery South. He was arrested by Jayhawkers in 1861 and narrowly escaped with his life because of a Unionist friend's intercession. Soon after his release, he left the Borderland and headed to California, but died enroute. Johnson's third living brother in the Borderland, Joseph, had a son who joined the Union Army.

Mattie's brother, **William Jackson Livingston,** engaged in guerrilla activities for the Confederacy near Hannibal, Missouri, attacking trains to cut off supplies and leading a band of Southerners. Livingston lived across the state in Marion County. At the outbreak of the war, Marion County was considered one of the most secessionist counties in the state. The county "was declared to be the South Carolina of Missouri" and one of its towns, Palmyra, "a miniature Charleston." When news of South Carolina's secession from the union arrived at Palmyra, the town went into high gear, organizing Confederate military units, stitching uniforms, and charging around the streets with great fervor. Livingston rented a farm near West Ely, 12 miles from Palmyra, and because he had military experience as a veteran of the Mexican War, was named Captain of a local Missouri State Guard unit.

Soon he achieved great notoriety as "Hawkeye Livingston," leader of a band of Confederate insurgents which numbered up to 50 men. On one occasion, he climbed to the top of a roof in Hannibal to determine the number of Federal troops in the town. He and leaders of some other insurgent bands considered an attack on these troops to regain control of Hannibal; Livingston's observation, however, was that there were too many Federal troops in town and advised the bands not to attack.

The St. Joseph Hannibal Railroad line was one of his chief military targets. Throughout 1861, Livingston's band harried trains making their way to Hannibal or St. Louis. During one of these episodes, two federal soldiers were killed.

In August, 1861, Livingston's band captured and killed Reverend Josiah Wheat, whom they suspected was a Federal spy. The old man was hung by Livingston's men and his body mutilated.

Civil War Loyalties Within Mattie's Circle

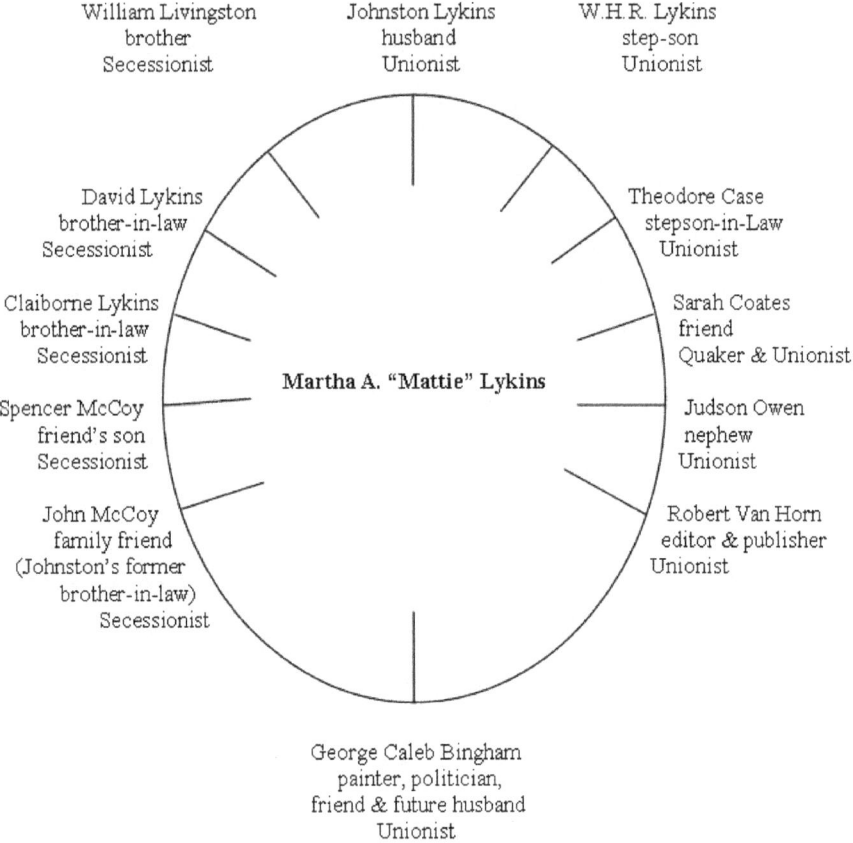

William Livingston
brother
Secessionist

Johnston Lykins
husband
Unionist

W.H.R. Lykins
step-son
Unionist

David Lykins
brother-in-law
Secessionist

Theodore Case
stepson-in-Law
Unionist

Claiborne Lykins
brother-in-law
Secessionist

Sarah Coates
friend
Quaker & Unionist

Martha A. "Mattie" Lykins

Spencer McCoy
friend's son
Secessionist

Judson Owen
nephew
Unionist

John McCoy
family friend
(Johnston's former
brother-in-law)
Secessionist

Robert Van Horn
editor & publisher
Unionist

George Caleb Bingham
painter, politician,
friend & future husband
Unionist

Eleven months later, Livingston was captured near Branson, Missouri, and detained at the military prison at Alton, Illinois. Livingston was found "not guilty" of three of the four charges, including the murder of Josiah Wheat, but was sentenced to be shot for violating acts of war. President Abraham Lincoln, however, declined to approve his death sentence, citing lack of evidence. In Kansas, Hawkeye and Mattie's brother, **Stephen J. Livingston,** maintained careful neutrality.

W. H. R. Lykins, Mattie's stepson, remained in Lawrence, Kansas and believed, along with his father, that a positive outcome for the region's future lay in its growth and development as a westward-looking entity, and that meant maintaining allegiance to the Union.

Mattie's Circle of Loyalties in Kansas City

Mattie's nephew, **Judson Owen**, soon found his medical skills to be in high demand. He left Mattie and Kansas City to become an assistant surgeon contracted by the Union Army to treat wounded soldiers on the battlefield.

Spencer McCoy, barely turned 18, left the military academy where he was a cadet in Virginia and rushed northward to join the fray in Missouri as a Confederate. As he complained to his father, he was armed with only a handgun, but, like many young men 18 years old, probably thought he was immortal and that war was a grand adventure.

Theodore Case, husband of Mattie's step-daughter Juliana, became a lieutenant in Van Horn's Union army and later rose to the position of Quartermaster; Sarah and Kersey Coates remained in the city, continuing to offer support and comfort to the community whenever they could. **Kersey Coates and Robert Van Horn,** officers in the Union Army and stalwart advocates for Kansas City, found themselves in hot water more than once for protecting friends and business associates who were suspected of being disloyal to the Union.

The husband of Mattie's other step-daughter, Sarah, was **Egbert F. Russell**, a photographer in the city. When Van Horn organized the Emergency Military Militia to protect Kansas City, Egbert enlisted, but held only a two month enlistment in the army.

George Caleb Bingham, born in 1811, was too old to serve in the Union Army, but he enlisted anyway. Mayor Van Horn used his influence to see to it that Bingham was appointed captain of the Home Guard and kept off the battlefield. From 1862-65, he served as State Treasurer and lived in Jefferson City.

John C. McCoy, Johnston's brother-in-law and Spencer McCoy's father, was suspected by the Union command of being disloyal to the Union. He was banned from Kansas City and relocated to Glasgow, a Missouri River town, for the duration of the war.

Nellie McCoy Harris, John C. McCoy's daughter, remained in the Kansas City area while waiting for the return of her husband, William Warren Harris, a surgeon for the Confederate Army. When her father and other Southern Sympathizers in Western Missouri were asked to gather up arms for Confederates at Independence, Nellie and a friend of her father's delivered them at great peril. One evening Nellie paid a visit to her cousin, Juliana Lykins Case, both of whom had babies. Juliana's husband, Theodore, offered to take care of the babies while their mothers chatted. In a very short time, he returned to them saying, "It won't work, girls. When I sing 'Yankee Doodle,' Nell's baby cries, and when I sing 'Dixie,' my baby howls, so I guess you'll have to keep them." Even as infants they were attuned to the tensions around them in the divided city. Mattie had, of course, watched both young mothers grow up and marry men on opposite sides in the war.

Kansas City residents, whether Northern or Southern in their sympathies, uncomfortably existed in the middle of the turmoil. Nellie McCoy Harris wrote:

I merely will tell how, in the main, we dwelt together in those stirring times. In the beginning we were so appalled by the "dreadful note of preparations" that we were in a manner crazed or stunned, and we discussed conditions freely with neighbors regardless of political predilections, but when our fathers, husbands or brothers buckled on their armor and tore themselves from home and loved ones, to join the army of their choice, fierce resentment against "the other side" supplanted for the moment the grief that had wrung our hearts. We sought solace in the hope and belief that our side would make short work of the war. . . .

The Northern element in our neighborhood asserted and firmly believed that Southern men, unaccustomed to physical effort, having slaves to perform the necessary labor, were lacking in stamina and too unaccustomed to hardships long to endure a soldier's life. The Southerners considered their loyal neighbors lacking in enthusiasm or profound sentiment, and as practical and dominated by the spirit of commercialism, to be willing long to continue a conflict that would necessarily play havoc with the nation's prosperity . . . .

Time proved how egregiously wrong were both. Sometimes neighbors, fearing criticism or censures from bitter partisans on their side, felt they must perform neighborly ministrations toward their foe friends secretly- but they did not fail to confer favors when needed, all the same.

In June, 1862, General Curtis, charged with keeping order in contentious Missouri, decided that guerrilla activities along the western border of Missouri had to be suppressed. He ordered the commander of each of the District of Missouri's subdivisions appoint a county board responsible for listing the names of all citizens in the area who were suspected of being disloyal. Then a schedule of assessments of these suspect citizens was established, prorated according to the wealth of the inhabitants, to pay for each Unionist killed, wounded or having property destroyed in raids. In Jackson County, one half of the assessment went to the militia and one half to destitute families of Union soldiers. Given the labyrinthine relationships existing in Kansas City among the citizens who had worked together for years to build Kansas City, the assessment was difficult to enforce. Enforcing the assessment would tear apart the fabric of Kansas City's social and business leadership. Among the names of the "disloyal" were W. H. Chick, A. B. H. McGee, Mrs. Benoist Troost and John Calvin McCoy. McCoy, revered by many as a founder of Kansas City, received the highest prorated assessment of all. As a result of the efforts of George Caleb Bingham and Kersey Coates, the assessment was never fully enforced.

Mattie Lykins was incensed by these assessments and the strictures of martial law. Because local newspapers had either been shut down or supplanted by strong radical Republican newspapers, Mattie's usual outlets for her writing were shut off. Not to be squelched, she decided to write to Col. Samuel Medary, editor of *The Crisis*, in Columbus, Ohio. Medary's stated purpose in publishing the newspaper was to undermine President Lincoln's administration, advocate for the Monroe Doctrine, ultra-States' Rights, and harmony among the states. Constant themes were denouncing the war, Lincoln's policies and the Union Army. Medary published Mattie's letter in March, 1863, after the hated assessments had rained down on more than two dozen alleged to be disloyal and they were imprisoned for refusing to pay. Mattie wrote of insults heaped on the citizenry:

> *I have witnessed unmitigated insults and outrages heaped upon some of our people. . . .Our husbands also, who have many of them gone gray in the service of their country, and have taken the Oath to support the Constitution more than a dozen times, and have*

*religiously observed it—are disarmed, their houses searched
from garret to cellar, and they are not allowed to retain
even an old shotgun to defend their wives and daughters
from the insults of negroes [those in the Union Army] and
brutal soldiers. . . . Upon the heels of this fifteen thousand
dollars comes another assessment of two hundred thousand
dollars. Inclosed [sic.] you will find the order to collect it at
once, also the card of nine of those who were arrested two
weeks ago.... When they come to collect the two hundred
thousand dollars, I think their prisons will run over with
the so-called disloyal. Some, I doubt not, will be sent to
breathe the foul air of "Camp Chase," Ohio.*[6]

The city lay paralyzed, in constant fear for residents' lives
and property. They watched helplessly as the population declined in
number by almost half, city services were largely unavailable, fires
raced unimpeded through warehouses, and property values
plummeted. The value of the citizenry's assets, including, no doubt,
those of the Lykins, lost half their value. In contrast, a rosy bloom
cast itself over their rival city, Leavenworth, as it prospered from the
war economy and the strangulation of Kansas City.

When the city fathers rallied in 1862 and reinstated the
Chamber of Commerce, they renewed their efforts to secure the
railroad for Kansas City. They held a fundraiser. The formerly cash-
flush city leaders strained to come up with money to support their
bid for the railroad's development. The Lykins, central as they were
to the effort, could barely afford to give $2.50 (about $55.00 in 2003
values) to the fundraising fair. The city's population forged on, its
commitment to the safety and well-being of their community
outweighing sectarian differences.

The death of John C. McCoy's son, Spencer Case McCoy,
embodied the complexities of the relationships among the citizens of
Kansas City and of the ability for human decency to transcend the
bitterness and division of the time. Spencer McCoy's military career
in the Confederacy was violently short. The poorly armed youth

was killed in his first military engagement at the second battle of Springfield. His father, hearing that the retreating Confederates were unable to bury their dead, drove a team and wagon 200 miles to the battlefield to bring his son home. Of the fifteen young men who had been buried in a mass grave by Union men, only Spencer was interred in a metal coffin. When John McCoy inquired of the Union officer in charge there, the man said that his wife and children had been without heat in Kansas City the winter before and reminded McCoy, who lived across the street from the family, that when he heard of their situation from his own children, he drove into the country and returned with a load of wood for them and a supply of provisions. In gratitude, this officer purchased a coffin and arranged a separate burial for the young man, marking the spot with a wooden cross bearing his name.

When McCoy brought Spencer back for burial in Union Cemetery, Spencer's sister wrote that the cortege following the coffin to the cemetery was "the most notable that had ever been seen in Kansas City. All bitterness was buried, political differences forgotten. Loyal and disloyal mingled their tears on this occasion." The community united to embrace their pioneer neighbor and friend.

In May, 1863, Mattie's brother, William Jackson Livingston, was arrested a second time in Hannibal and charged with spying. A few months later, Livingston wrote to the Provost Marshall requesting that his trial date be set as soon as possible. Mattie never mentioned this brother in her journal; however, in her scrapbook there is a letter from one of her critics which alludes to his hanging.

Whether the Union commanders overseeing martial law in Kansas City or her friends in Kansas City knew of his connection to Mattie is unknown. Still, his arrest was undoubtedly another sorrowful event for Mattie.

In 1863, the military command over Western Missouri was led by Kansan General Thomas Ewing. He was extremely frustrated at his inability to quell the guerrillas in the region and decided on a strategy of depriving guerrillas of their support network (primarily family members and friends in the area) by arresting and relocating family members to other states and cities.

In addition, he announced that all guerrillas captured were to be summarily executed. Ewing "began a policy of arresting and imprisoning the sisters of known guerrillas.

Ewing used their alleged 'spying' as a pretext for these illegal arrests, and the women were held without trial, bail, or legal recourse." After arrest, they were incarcerated in a makeshift prison at 1425 Grand Avenue (about the middle of the block on the east side of Grand Avenue) in downtown Kansas City. [This makeshift prison for Southern women was one of the commercial buildings pictured below. Today (2011), the Sprint Arena occupies this historic block.]

When the building that Ewing commandeered from George Caleb Bingham (unbeknownst to Bingham, who was serving as Provisional State Treasurer in Jefferson City, Missouri) collapsed, four of the young women were killed. Among the dead was a sister of "Bloody" Bill Anderson, a notorious guerrilla. Another sister sustained injuries which made her an invalid for the rest of her short life. Citizens and soldiers rushed to the scene of the collapsed building to rescue the women trapped there. Mattie Lykins was at the scene that afternoon. She later wrote:

> One hot day, Friday, August 14th, about two o'clock, this prison fell, burying beneath its walls a number of its inmates, four of whom were dreadfully mangled and crushed to death. . . . In less than an hour after this building fell, I was informed by some of the women prisoners that they had repeatedly been told by the guards that this house was giving away and would eventually fall. "But," they said, "we had so often been told during our imprisonment equally as alarming stories which proved false that we paid no attention to this one: yet every few days, we heard the building crack, which was invariable followed by the falling of pieces of plastering from the ceiling."
> Doctor Joshua Thorne . . . was at that time chief surgeon of the hospital at this place. While I stood beside him near the building, watching the removal of the living and the dead from the debris, some one remarked to him that they supposed some of the soldiers on guard would be found buried beneath the ruins. "No," replied Doctor Thorne, "Not a bluecoat will be found; every man who has been detailed to stand guard at this prison for the last few weeks knew the house to be unsafe and have kept themselves at a safe distance from the trembling walls. I knew the building to be unsafe," he continued, "and notified the military authorities of the fact, and suggested the removal of the women prisoners, but my suggestion was not heeded. Before you is the result."

The deaths and injuries caused by the Union Jail's collapse enraged the guerrilla forces. In addition, Ewing had ordered that any captured guerilla was to be shot on the spot. These two events triggered Quantrill's attack on Lawrence, Kansas, the following week.

Quantrill called together his captains, Bill Anderson among them, to agree on a plan to attack Lawrence, a site where he believed the most property stolen from taken and where the greatest revenge could be exacted. Quantrill and 194 men rode into Lawrence at dawn on August 20; by the end of their massacre, "some 150 male inhabitants of Lawrence were killed in the raid, and much of the town was burned to the ground. On August 23, 1863, *The Leavenworth Daily Conservative* reported the loss to the town as two million dollars in property and two hundred thousand dollars in cash. It described Massachusetts Street, the main business artery, as 'one mass of smouldering ruins and crumbling walls. . . . Only two business houses were left upon the street–one known as the Armory and the other the old Miller block. . . . About one hundred and twenty-five houses in all were burned, and only one or two escaped being ransacked, and everything of value carried away or destroyed.'"

W. H. R. Lykins' house was not touched. In the anger and confusion that followed the raid, he and his step-mother, Mattie, came under suspicion as being involved in orchestrating the raid. A historian, Burton Williams, later explored an accusation against them made by Rev. Hugh D. Fisher, Methodist Minister, and a man of questionable credibility. As a free-stater, Fisher had quickly been appointed Chaplain of James H. Lane's Fifth Kansas cavalry, and he immediately engaged in freeing slaves and helping himself to Missourians' property; further, he had previously gotten into difficulty with other clergy, mishandled church funds and was "cited as a fraud and a liar." In his papers, Fisher claimed:

> *Spies were in town all night . . . indeed it is placed beyond peradventure that the mother of a certain Banker of Lawrence, who secured all his valuables the night before the raid, spent weeks with his family in Lawrence, and made a map of the town giving the names, residences, and location of those who were to be killed and their homes burned, marking them thus–"Kill and Burn," or "Burn" and if the property belonged to a sympathizer only "Kill."*

This map was taken by this heinous woman [Mattie Lykins] to Kansas City, and Quantrill and his lieutenants were entertained day and night in the greatest seclusion in her parlor, where they had the maps explained preparatory to the sacking of Lawrence.

When this claim appeared in published form, Fisher went further: "An old Mrs. L-----, of Kansas City, was the spy who furnished the necessary information and map of Lawrence . . . the torch was applied to every house that had been marked on the traitoress' map."

Williams cited other historians' claims that Lykins and his home were passed over because Sallie Young, a resident of Lawrence, asked that specific persons not be touched, some saying Sallie was a conspirator and others claiming that she was heroically saving others on that day.

Williams concluded that the evidence against Lykins and his step-mother was circumstantial, citing Lykins southern background, his Kansas City roots, and Lykins' own acknowledgment that he knew some of the raiders, but Williams also raised questions regarding the survival of Lykins' home and the sparing of his life in the neighborhood where the worst destruction occurred. Finally he noted that Lykins received restitution for losses suffered during the raid, wondering whether the "destruction of property [was] brought on by his own complicity or that of his mother."

Mattie maintained her innocence throughout her life. In her journal account of that day in Lawrence, she wrote that she took her three-year old grand-daughter with her to visit her step-son and his family in Lawrence, arriving on the evening before the raid. When she asked W. H. R. about the news of the day, he reported that the commander at Fort Leavenworth had announced that Quantrill had left the Borderland and gone South.

As a result, the men of Lawrence had been directed to stack their arms in the arsenal and get some rest. "We have had a hard time of it this summer," William said. "We have stood our guard every night for months and we were beginning to feel pretty well used up for want of rest from drill and guard duties."

As Mattie prepared for bed she heard gunfire and when she asked about it, William told her that Captain Jennison had been forming a new regiment and that the troops who were camping near the town drilled in the late evening and early morning to avoid the heat and then concluded their drills by firing their rifles. As a result, when Mattie heard gunfire and saw men riding in the streets at dawn, she was not alarmed. When she saw a man running away from the men on horseback, she awakened her daughter-in-law, who sleepily responded, "Oh, those fellows belong to Jennison's regiment. They are just riding about in the cool of the morning for fun." Then Mattie saw the horsemen kill a man going to work and she awakened William :

> *Mr. Lykins [William H. R.], who was sleeping in another room, was about the last person in the house to be made acquainted with the appalling situation. Throwing on his clothes he started for the door with the hope of making an escape into a cornfield near by. By this time the guerrillas had surrounded his house and were guarding every avenue of escape. I told him that escape was impossible and that his safety depended on his remaining in the house. Still, he insisted on making the attempt, fearing he would do so, with all the physical strength I had, I held him back and by dint force and argument succeeded in getting him back into his room. I then locked the door and put the key in my pocket. It was thus that he escaped death.*

Were Mattie and William involved in the planning of the raid on Lawrence? Anything is possible, of course. However, it defies the imagination that a grandmother would be so irresponsible and ghoulish as to knowingly bring a three-year-old grandchild into such a dangerous and ugly situation. Indeed, she would have stayed away herself both for her safety and, if she were indeed a co-conspirator,

66

to avoid suspicion. Further, Fisher's accusation does not match up with what is known of other aspects of Mattie's character.

Although Mattie was an articulate Southern sympathizer, she spent her life taking up the causes of children, whether through educating them or through establishing a home for Confederate orphans. An orphan herself, she would not likely have wanted to see other children made orphans.

The prominence of her husband and his good friend George Caleb Bingham, and their ardent stances against secession and having the Borderland devastated by violence make it unlikely, too, that she would have been plotting the raid while entertaining Quantrill in her parlor. The historian, Williams, pointed out that C. E. Lewis, writing to his brother from Franklin, Kansas, a few days after the Lawrence raid stated that there was a map and that, "Names and houses were marked prior to their coming in." Lewis did not assert, however, that Mrs. Lykins was the creator of this map, as Fisher had intimated.

An assertion by Mattie's nephew, Alphonse Hughes, however, does muddy the waters. Alphonse told Eugene Ferguson (one of Johnston Lykins' nephews) that he lived with Mattie at the time of the raid on Lawrence and that Mattie and Johnston were nearly hanged for providing information about individuals in Lawrence.[7]

It is possible that in the feverish rage of the moment, Mattie knew that guerillas were threatening to attack Lawrence in reprisal and that she asked them not to harm people she cared about there. That is different from saying that she was part of a plot or was aware of the date or plan of attack.

Order No. 11 Issued

Following the attack on Lawrence, Ewing issued "General Orders No. 11," commonly called "Order No. 11," to satisfy Missouri and Kansas Unionist demands that the bushwhackers be stopped and to forestall criticism from Washington, D.C. (Jim Lane, a Kansas leader in Lawrence, had influence with Abraham Lincoln.) Written and signed at the historic Pacific House Hotel (still standing as of 2011 in the River Market area of downtown Kansas City), the edict stated:

> All persons living in Jackson, Cass, and Bates Counties, Missouri, and in that part of Vernon included in this district, except those living within 1 mile of the limits of Independence, Hickman Mills, Pleasant Hill, and Harrisonville, And except those in that part of Kaw Township, Jackson County, North of Brush Creek and west of the Big Blue, are hereby ordered to remove from their present places of residence within fifteen days from the date hereof . . . Officers commanding companies and detachments serving in the counties named will see that this paragraph is promptly obeyed.

Historically, the idea of forcibly removing citizens who support the enemy was a common practice of military forces trying to suppress rebellion and guerrilla warfare. "General William Halleck, general in chief of the U.S. Army, assured Ewing that the measure fell 'within the recognized laws of war." Halleck, however, did not agree with Ewing's method of implementing the order. Ewing assigned Kansas soldiers, full of anger and bent on revenge, to enforce the order. Ewing may have made this assignment of Kansas troops in deference to Jim Lane.

Castel, writing 100 years after the implementation of Order No. 11, described it as "the most drastic and repressive military measure directed against civilians by the Union Army during the Civil War. In fact, with the exception of the hysteria-motivated herding of Japanese-Americans into concentration camps during World War II, it stands as the harshest treatment ever imposed on United States citizens under the plea of military necessity in our nation's history."

A leading critic of the order was a prominent political figure and painter, George Caleb Bingham, whose Unionist credentials were impeccable. Bingham demanded that Order 11 be rescinded, but his desire was not to be fulfilled. The painter furiously vowed that he would use his artistic powers to show the nation how despicable he believed General Ewing to be. Bingham worked from his studio, which was at the time adjacent to his home in Independence, Missouri (today, it is the house museum, the Bingham-Waggoner Estate, officially, the Lewis-Bingham-Waggoner Estate). There he created one of his most well-known paintings, "Order No. 11" to exact his revenge. His rage and his determination to destroy Ewing's reputation and political aspirations lasted until the end of his life.

Between 1865 and 1868, Bingham created an impressive 6' x 8' painting which he titled, "Martial Law" (it quickly became popularly named and known as, "Order No. 11"). It was painted on a gingham tablecloth. Bingham used this painting and its subsequent, widely-distributed engraving, as his weapon of choice in publicizing the horrors of the military action. [Reproductions of an original Sartain engraving, signed by Bingham, are available for sale from the Jackson County Historical Society.]

The painting shows Ewing, cold and detached, supervising troops in the process of removing a Missouri family from its home. Castel describes the scene of the painting:

> A Kansas Red Leg has just shot down a young man, and another is about to shoot the elderly head of the family, oblivious to the pleas of a beautiful young woman kneeling at his feet. The house is being pillaged by Union

69

soldiers, one of whom bears a likeness to the noted jayhawker, Colonel Charles Jennison. In the background columns of smoke rise from burning fields and a long funereal line of refugees wends its way along the road.

The child clinging to that elderly man's leg is Bingham's son, Rollins, as attributed in his own words:

[I] *well remember posing often in that old studio for the figure of the little boy clasping the knee of the aged man menaced by the sinister "red leg." The pose was assisted by a wooden mannequin that took the part of the old man. The picture represents no facial likeness of* [Rollins] *at the time, but only the attitude.*[8]

Later, George Caleb Bingham's studio was on the third floor of the building on the southwest corner of 3rd and Main Streets in downtown Kansas City.

There, between 1870 and 1876, Bingham painted a second copy, or version of "Martial Law," or, "Order No. 11." According to

Rollins Bingham, *"it was intended as a living memorial in case of untoward destruction of the original. I have my father's often repeated statement well in memory that this replica, while an exact reproduction, was to his own mind really a better picture than the original and more likely to stand the wear and tear of years."*[9]

Some have claimed that the man with a hat sitting horseback just behind the elderly man was a self-portrait of George Caleb Bingham. Maybe. Maybe not.

The only other positively identifiable *"intentional likeness"* of an historical figure in "Order No. 11," according to Rollins Bingham, was that of General Thomas Ewing, *"the mounted officer in the middle background face to the left, before the plundered mansion."*

One of the victims of Order No. 11 was Martin Rice, a Unionist farmer near Lone Jack, Jackson County, Missouri, who wrote an 1865 account of his experience. His account is remarkably measured, given the amount of suffering he endured:

> *It* [Order No. 11] *is often spoken of and referred to, and has been much condemned by some and strenuously defended by others; and while I shall not attempt to do one or the other, I will, as plainly, concisely and impartially as I can, describe what I saw, witnessed and felt of its incidents, consequences, and results, without pretending to say or to know whether the consequences would have been better or worse if that order had never been made and enforced.*[10]

Rice obtained his certificate of loyalty, but the next day was arrested by soldiers of the Kansas 9th Regiment along with his son, son-in-law, and five neighbor men ranging in age from 17-75. After being marched to an encampment about three quarters of a mile away, a Kansas military officer appeared and took down the names of the eight men, retired a short distance away with some of his men, and allowed the prisoners to sit down by a fence. Soon, the officer reappeared and directed Rice to take his son and leave immediately; the others were not allowed to go. Rice wrote,

71

We immediately left as commanded, leaving our friends and neighbors behind, never to see them in life again: for in a very short time after reaching home, the report of several guns, in quick succession, alarmed us still more. . . . Miss Jane Cave heroically repaired to the spot and found the company gone, and the six prisoners all dead, some of them pierced with many balls. . . .Of neighbors left in the county, there were none that I knew of, except the families of the men who had just been killed. Nobody left to bury them but me and my son, and my old neighbor Mr. Hunter. . . . My aged friend and neighbor, at the age of three score and Fifteen, helping me with his own hands to lay his two sons, his only sons, his grandson, and son-in-law, with two other relatives (one of whom was my son-in-law), in the rude and shallow grave that our own hands had dug for them.

It may, perhaps, be asked why or for what cause this bloody tragedy was enacted; why it was that these men were killed, and that I was spared. They were all quiet, peaceable citizens, none of them had borne arms against the government, except David Hunter, a few days at the very first, at Camp Holloway, and he had afterward done duty in the enrolled militia (Union forces). True, they were all Southern men, and Southern sympathizers; and some of them had sons in the Southern army. I thought then, and still think, the principal cause were that Quantrill and his raiders, on their way to Lawrence, stopped and ate supper on the Potter farm, and that some of these men visited them while they were getting that supper.

The citizens in the western Missouri counties fled the area however they could–crowding onto steamboats, walking, and riding oxen (most horses had been confiscated).

Among those forced to evacuate were President Harry S Truman's maternal grandparents, who lived on a farm they had purchased from Johnston Lykins when they settled in Missouri. For them, it was the crowning indignation. In her reparations claim of 1902, Harriet Louisa Young, Truman's grandmother, stated that the Young farm had been pillaged five times by Union forces, beginning with those of Jim Lane in 1861. The total damage claimed by Harriet was around $21,442 (more than a half million dollars in today's monetary equivalent). Although Harry Truman's grandfather had signed a loyalty oath more than a year earlier, the family complied with Order No. 11 and left the farm, permitted to take a wagonload of possessions. Truman's mother, Martha Ellen, was among those "trudging northward on a hot, dusty road behind the swaying wagon, headed for 'bitter exile' in Kansas City."[11]

Mattie's Expulsion from Kansas City

And where *was* the intrepid Mattie Lykins in all this?
Right in the middle of it, of course.

Mattie was one of those residents of Kansas City who was forced to leave the area because of her outspoken support of the South and, possibly, because of the accusations which had been made against her regarding the Lawrence raid.

To carry out General Orders No. 11, Major P. B. Plumb, who presided over the "District of the Border," signed the following removal order, which included "Mrs. Dr. Lykins." (See fourth name in the list on page 76.)

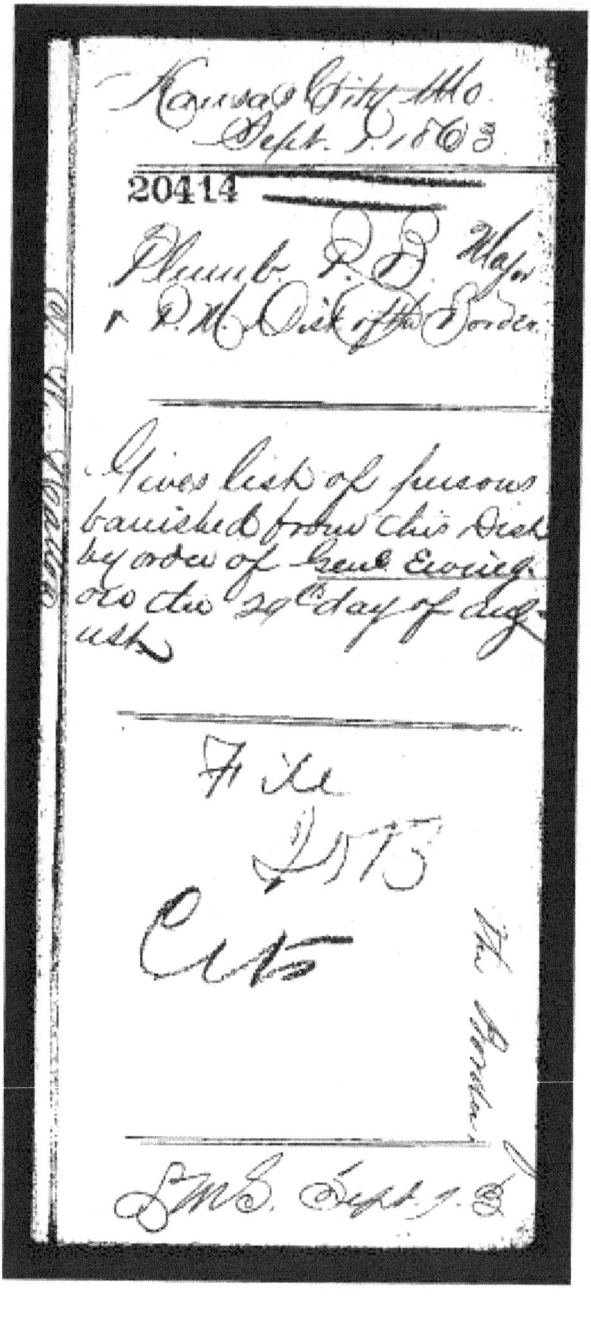

Kansas City Mo.
Sept. 7. 1863

20414

Plumb P. B. Major
r P. M. Dist of the Border.

Gives list of persons
banished from this Dist
by order of Genl Ewing
on the 29th day of Aug-
ust

File

Cts

L.W.S. Sept. 1.

74

Kansas City, Mo. Sept. 1st 1863

Col. J. O. Broadhead,
Pro. Mar. Gen.

Sir:—

On the 29th. day of August
I issued the following order, towit:—

"Special Orders.   "Head Quarters District of the Border
No. 64   } Extract.—   "Kansas City, Mo. August 29. 1863.

"Jesse Riddlesbarger and family, residents of
"Kansas City, Mo. are ordered to remove from this District within ten days
"from the date hereof. They will not go to the Counties of Platte, Clay, Ray or
"Carroll, Missouri to reside, nor return to this district, during the rebellion
"without previous express permission from competent military authority.

"By Order of Brig. Gen. Ewing.
"P. B. Plumb,
"Major and Pro. Marshal."

On that day I also issued similar
orders to the following persons, towit:—

~~Nelson Holmes~~ of Kansas City
R. H. Nelson, and family of

75

William Gillis of Kansas City

James Sweeney and family . . . "

Reuben Garnett and family . . . .

~~Willoughby Stevens and family~~

Mrs. T. Lyskins . . .

Richard Hardesty and family . . .

Mr. Charles Kendall — . , .

Mrs. Ruth Chipman — . . .

George Nicholson — . . ,

T. W. Chick and wife — . . "

Hollon Rice and family of Osage Co. Kansas

Montague Rice — . , . "

Miss Alice Sanetter — of Olathe, Kansas.

Mrs. Ross ———— of Independence Mo.

Mrs. Tillery — . , . "

Mrs. O'Donnel — , . "

Mrs. Smar and family . . . "

Mrs. Tom Maxwell — , " . "

Mrs. Silby — . . "

Mrs. Fannie Haines — , " . "

Miss Mary Jane Irwin — , " . "

Mrs. Hall and family — . " . ,,

76

Mrs. Saml. H. Woodson ———— of Independence Mo.

Mrs. Ashley ————,

Mrs. McCready ————,

John Eagin and family.

Mr. Thorriston and family.

Mr. Shore and family.

R. C. Runyan and family.

Wash. Campbell and family.

Samuel Hanley and wife.

Mr. See and family.

Mr. Cashinberry and wife.

Mr. Neat and family.

On Sept. 1. Similar orders were issued to the following residents of Kansas City Mo. to wit.

Richard R. Ferguson and family (not including Felix Ferguson)

W. G. Barkley and family.

John W. Summers and family.

P. T. Scruggs.

Mrs. Mary Thorst;

Ben Jaudon and family.

Mr. Donahue and family.

William M. Wiley;

B. D. Smith and family
Asa Maddox and family
Semuel Hall, wife and family
Wm. Gilpin and family
Thomas Aspling and family
Oliver P. Burnes
S. W. Hatton
Hezekiah Holmes and family
Joseph McDougal
Phillip D. Pollard
Dr. A. J. Peirce.

I am Very Respectfully
Your Obt. Servt.

R. W. Hand

As she stood on the deck of a steamboat leaving the city, her husband and, possibly, George Caleb Bingham, watched her depart. (Both her husband and her friend were anti-secessionists who had official capacities–Johnston as a city councilman and Bingham, then living in Jefferson City, but in Kansas City on business.) A Kansas citizen, Daniel Geary, was an eye-witness:

> Mrs. Lykins, a talented and accomplished woman for those days and a writer of short stories, was banished during the war by the military authorities for disloyalty to the government.
> I remember the incident well, as when the ferry boat upon which she took passage to the distant shores of Clay County where she was to abide, was leaving the wharf, she was calling to the doctor where he would find his underwear, and "To be sure they were quite dry" before he put them on, etc.

When Ewing's successor permitted "loyal" citizens to return to Kansas City in January, 1864, Mattie returned from eastern Missouri where she had gone after her expulsion from her home. When she was greeted by her friend, Col. Kersey Coates, she said with her usual spark, "Here I am, Colonel, twice as big as life and twice as natural."

The fury of Order No. 11 devastated the countryside around Kansas City. In Cass County, there were only 600 people of a population of 10,000 who were still there as of September 9, 1863. In Bates County, the population loss was so great that there was no infrastructure left for conducting business transactions or legal procedures until after the war. Throughout the border counties, burned out shells of farmsteads, homes and plantations were all that remained on the once prosperous, well-kept lands. Livestock abandoned to the wild foraged for food in the region now known as "The Burnt District."

Mattie's brother, William Jackson Livingston, stood trial in the Summer of 1864, and he was found guilty and sentenced to hang. Livingston's case was followed nation-wide by the press: on August 26, 1864, a Lowell, Massachusetts newspaper reported that his sentence had been carried out:

> *Execution of a Spy.*—Mr. Jackson Livingston of Marion county, Missouri, was hung last Friday in the jail yard of St. Louis as a spy. He protested his innocence to the last. He joined the Catholic Church shortly before his execution and met his fate with as much apparent composure as if he was starting on a pleasant journey. He left a wife and four children. His wife was present at the execution.

While Ewing and the Union military commanders or her friends and neighbors may not have known of the connection between Mattie and William J. Livingston, her brother's notoriety was surely an additional source of sorrow for Mattie and, potentially, an endangerment to her safety.

Mattie's brother had been executed only two months earlier when word came to Kansas City that General Sterling Price was headed toward Kansas City in a last-ditch effort to gain a stronghold in Missouri. In October, 1864, Confederate General Price, having determined that the garrisons at Jefferson City and St. Louis were too strong for him to take, headed toward Kansas City. Disease and desertion had reduced his force from 12,000 to 8,500. Hearing of Price's coming, Union commanders called their forces in to defend Kansas City: 10,000 troops from nearby Ft. Leavenworth and 12,000 from St. Louis. Sterling Price's troops fought a good fight, but they were seriously out-numbered and under-equipped from the outset. Price had no choice but retreat to Arkansas and, for the duration of the war, posed no further threat to Kansas City.

Mattie, in the meantime, rolled up her sleeves and worked side by side with her loyalist Quaker friend, Sarah Coates, as they tended to the wounded brought to McGee's hotel for care. In the face of this human suffering, sectarian loyalties simply did not matter to these two women who were Kansas Citians and lifelong friends.

McGEE'S HOTEL ON GRAND AVENUE.

When Mattie wrote about the war years in her journal years later, she reflected:

It is not my purpose here to discuss the right or wrong of that dreadful conflict, nor to drag from the grave of the past the bitter, lingering remembrances of those sad days. But we should forever bear in remembrance the time when our fields were ruined and our homes desolated. The anguish of broken hearts, the cries of the widow and fatherless, the pain and suffering of the crippled and maimed on both sides as an indelible warning on the pages of memory never again to resort to the sword and torch as the arbitrators of our sectional disputes. Often during the war it really seemed to me that Kansas City got more than her share of the bitterness of the strife. The daily tread of thousands of soldiers in our streets, the alarming reports of the invasion of our state by the Confederate army, the harrowing telegraphic dispatches of the dreadful slaughter of the contending armies, the harassing and daily warfare carried on in our county between the Kansas Jayhawkers and the Missouri Bushwhackers kept us in a state of alarm and excitement for four years without a day's intermission.

Mattie and the Kansas City community survived the war, but barely. The patchwork quilt comprising this early city was tattered and worn, the threads holding its diverse pieces together pulled and strained, the patches frayed and discolored. The war had taken a dreadful toll on the energy and vitality of Kansas City's citizens and they, Mattie and Johnston included, were exhausted. They were now faced with repairing the damage and building a future.

CHAPTER 4

An Overabundance of Losses

When the Civil War finally ended, family crises took the place of the daily anxieties created by living under martial law. Two of Mattie's step-granddaughters, Martha and Emily (Bella) Case, died in 1865. Mattie Case, her step-grandmother's namesake, was the little girl who was in Lawrence, Kansas, with her step-grandmother on the day of Quantrill's Raid. She, followed by her sister, became ill quite suddenly, both dying within days. Mattie wrote in memory of her little namesake, "Alas her light step will be heard no more, her laughing voice is hushed in death. . . . She came like a bright and beautiful vision, and brought with her joy and gladness, and each day unfolded another and yet another charm which bound her to her parents' hearts."

In addition to mourning the deaths of the two little girls, the family continued to suffer personal losses. Two of Johnston's children experienced life-changing crises in 1868 and it is likely that Johnston and Mattie needed to provide both financial and child-care support for a period of time. An article in *The Leavenworth Daily Commercial* noted that William's mental health was causing great concern: "We learn from *The Kansas Journal* that Mr. W. H. R. Lykins, a prominent Banker of Lawrence, and last year Mayor of that city, is deranged, and while laboring under a fit of insanity, attempted self-destruction. Misfortune in business has led to this distressing event, and his friends are said to entertain great fears for him in the future." The Banking House of W. H. R. Lykins failed in 1868 and William left Lawrence to live in Kansas City. His business failure resulted in his working as a clerk. In the long term, this less high-powered work allowed him to pursue his true passion:

scholarship. He became a widely published writer of articles on geology and archeology, sending archaeological reports to the Smithsonian; however, he must have needed some emotional and financial support while he regained equilibrium.

Around 1868, too, Mattie's older step-daughter, Sarah Lykins Russell, was divorced by her husband of eighteen years. Her husband departed for Texas and Sarah was left to support seven children ranging in age from 17 to 1; although she regularly published serialized stories and poems, she probably did not make enough money to support this large family on her own.

Several deaths in the family occurred between 1869 and 1873: Juliana and Theodore Case lost a third daughter, four-year old Olive, leaving a daughter and two sons still living. Between 1869 and 1870, Mattie's sister Elizabeth Owen lost both her husband, William, and a son, Judson, who died at the age of 32, leaving a wife and children in Kentucky. In 1872, The Case children's mother, Juliana, also died. Mattie stayed at her step-daughter's side as she weakened and died, and provided care to the three remaining Case children. In Juliana's obituary, the writer, probably Mattie or Juliana's sister Sarah, reflected on the beauty of her spirit:

> *Ever kind and affectionate, she was loved as few can be loved. In 1851, and when about twelve years of age, she became the step-daughter of the present Mrs. Dr. Lykins, for whom she formed the most ardent and undying attachment, reciprocated by love equally strong on the part of her adopted mother, a relation so happy that not a single event ever occurred to mar it, and when death came to tear this loved one away, no one, save her dear husband, clung to her with more ardent love and affection, nor felt the anguish and grief of a torn and bleeding heart more intensely than did that stricken mother. . . .When asked by her weeping mother if she had any request to leave, she said, "Take care of my babies."*

Juliana's death came a few months after the death of another of Mattie's step-granddaughters, Effie Russell. Within months of Juliana's death, the family lost Sarah Russell's only son, Willie. In April, 1873, his grieving mother wrote of her daughter, sister and son:

> *Dear household angels, other hearts may change;*
> *Earth's truest ones may falter or forget,*
> *But naught hath power to shadow or estrange*
> *The love whereon death's sacred seal is set.*
> *Like hoarded jewels, memory shall keep*
> *Each dear familiar smile, and look, and tone,*
> *Till I shall come to share they dreamless sleep,*
> *And walk no more life's weary ways alone.*

For the modern reader, the concept of losing so many young family members to disease within an eight-year period is hard to grasp. The numbers of children's deaths in the 1870s are difficult for us to imagine enduring. In the last 150 years, the theory of germs as a cause for disease, the development of antibiotics and vaccinations, sophisticated surgical methods, and the understanding of sanitation methodologies have all, mercifully, shielded contemporary Americans from the number and frequency of losses sustained by Mattie's family.

In addition to the deaths and crises shaking the family to its foundation, the economy wreaked havoc with their finances. In the late 1860s and early 1870s, tumultuous economic conditions dominated the lives of businessmen and farmers in the region, and both Johnston Lykins and his son, William, were caught up in these economic difficulties.

Speculation abounded in the post-war environment, particularly in railroads. Industry and trade had boomed during the first years after the war. By 1873, railroad mileage had doubled since 1860, and this rapid expansion was a prolific cause of rash speculation. While business was expanding, the currency was contracting. Paper money had depreciated and the conditions were ripe for a crash. A severe financial depression swept through the country following the failure of Jay Cooke and Co., a banking firm financing the Northern Pacific Railroad. Speculators invested with abandon in the post-war environment until an October day ushered in the "Panic of 1873."

Johnston Lykins' assets had already been eroded during the martial law years when business came to a halt in Kansas City. Even though he was president of the Mechanics Bank of Kansas City, he was not exempted from the effects of the rampant speculation and ensuing panic. His wealth destroyed, he was forced into bankruptcy the following year.

Confederate Widows and Orphans

The suffering of the Lykins in the post-Civil War period was not unique. The soldiers of the Confederacy and their families struggled with the loss of their health and livelihoods. When the soldiers returned to civilian life in Missouri, there were no safety nets for them, and members of the now dominant Unionist society could not easily forget the pain and loss suffered within their own ranks.

Mattie Lykins saw the war's aftermath of deprivation and suffering around her and advocated for the many voiceless men, women and children left destitute and vulnerable.

Motivated by the suffering and injustice she saw and ever supportive of the underdog, she wrote to President Andrew Johnson in 1866, imploring him to grant clemency to William Maddox, a man she believed was wrongly accused of participating in Quantrill's raid of Lawrence three years earlier.[12] Because of her large network of friends, many of whom had come from the South, it is also entirely possible that she knew the Maddox family and was responding to their grief. The 24-year old man's' trial was moved to Olathe, Kansas, to prevent his lynching in Lawrence, and, indeed, he would have been lynched there as well had not the citizens of Olathe been certain that he would be tried, found guilty and hung. When Maddox was able to produce witnesses to prove that he was not in Lawrence at the time of the massacre, he was acquitted. The acquittal must have angered and frustrated Kansas residents, because he was a trusted member of Quantrill's band and had engaged actively in other guerilla activities.

Mattie was particularly moved by the sorry plight of the Confederates' widows and orphans, many of whom had no sources of support or aid as they fought to survive in an indifferent, if not hostile, environment. That year, she and several women friends in Kansas City began a campaign to establish a home for widows and orphans of Confederate soldiers. In a letter to the Editor of *The Republican*, July 11, 1866, Mattie explained their purpose:

> Permit me through your columns to announce to the suffering widows and orphans of Southern soldiers from Missouri who perished in the late war that the ladies of Kansas City and Jackson County are organizing a society for the maintenance and education of the widows and orphans of the persons alluded to. The design is to establish a parent society in Kansas City, and to invite the formation and co-operation of auxiliary societies in all of the counties of the State, in order to raise a fund for the founding of an orphan asylum and home for the destitute of our own bereaved and helpless sufferers, to be located in this city.

In this time, emotions were still raw from the trauma of the past five years, so in taking on the humanitarian effort, Mattie, always controversial, was criticized. Beneath the headline, "A Disgraceful Letter," a detractor wrote:

> The following disgraceful letter appeared in the St. Louis *Republican* of yesterday. Being written by a lady, we have no comment to make. It will, however, be pardonable to also state that we think the writer ought to be largely reorganized, fully reconstructed and let the Confederate dead, who have been properly killed and decently interred, alone. The writer of the letter was banished from this city, as a secessionist; has always been a consistent, outspoken rebel and is the sister of a man who was executed by the U.S. authorities, as a spy, during the war.

Indeed, Mattie had first-hand knowledge of the suffering of the wives and children of Confederate dead, not only from her first-hand observation of the bereft families in Kansas City, but also, quite possibly, from knowing of the plight of her dead brother's family. In 1863, he had written from Gratiot Prison to the Provost Marshall to ask for the money taken from him at the time of his arrest: *"General I would like very much to have the money for my family dependent on me for a support and are now suffering. For something to live. And are very destitute of cloth. If I had the money it would be a great relief to me and my family."* Livingston's family moved near his brother, Stephen J. Livingston, right after the war both, undoubtedly, to escape the notoriety of their dead father's hanging and to seek food and shelter.

A writer in a subsequent letter defended Mattie and the committee's work, saying "This is commendable, for however great may have been the error of these deluded and mistaken men Christianity teaches us to care for the widow and the orphan irrespective of the causes which produced their unhappy condition. There is a moral beauty and heroism in such efforts, which when the passions of the hour shall have passed away, will be recognized and appreciated by every being possessed of a human heart."

In one of her appeals, Mattie pointed out that individuals and organizations had gone around the state to seek support for the education and maintenance of Southern orphans, "but, thus far, not one dollar has been set aside for the relief and education of the suffering ones of Missouri." She described the desperate situation of women and children:

And now, the clash of arms is heard no more, their cry for bread comes from every desolate and waste place throughout our State–Again and again we hear of mothers toiling in the fields; others with less health and strength, but burdened with the care of children are occupying a servant place in strangers' kitchens. Not only this, but from their ragged tents and pallets of straw, they plead in piteous accents for a shelter from the coming winter.

The original 1867 Confederate Widows' and Orphans' Home, which burned on August 11, 1873

Area newspapers carried numerous reports of fund-raising events such as a grand ball: "The Ex-Confederates, their friends and sympathizers, contemplate giving a free dinner in this city on the 27th of October. . . . General Beauregard is expected. Ten thousand people or more will be present. Grand ball at night, the net proceeds of which will be donated to the Widows' and Orphans' Home of Kansas City, Mo. Admission to ball–Two dollars."

The women tried various approaches to raising funds for the home, and responded to critics that their work was a humanitarian rather than partisan effort. In making an appeal for funds, Mattie wrote:

> We believe that even the veriest enemies of the South would not take the responsibility of opposing so noble an enterprise. Their animosity does not reach beyond the grave, nor to the widow and orphan of the brave dead. They will bid us Godspeed in this benevolent undertaking; and many will give of their abundance to this "Home" for the widow and fatherless. They will see in it no political or individual distinction; no desire to renew the strife and bitterness of feeling which has filled our land, but simply a desire to do good–to save from ruin the truly friendless, and a desire to offend neither heaven nor earth.

A critic of the effort to secure funds for the widows' and orphans' home bitterly suggested that the fundraising committee direct its efforts toward providing a decent burial for the Confederate dead in the city. Mattie tartly replied that the matter was being taken care of and, indeed, she did see to it that a corner in the Union Cemetery was reserved as a burial site honoring them.

Appeal of Orphans' Home Society!

187?

At a meeting of the Trustees of the Widows' and Orphans' Home, called by the President, to consider the best course to pursue in view of the disastrous fire on the 11th of August, which resulted in the total destruction of the Home, and the turning out of doors of its inmates, with the loss of much of their clothing, bedding, furniture, &c., it was *Resolved*, that the ladies managing the Institution be advised to proceed without delay to rebuild so much of it as is absolutely necessary for the shelter and comfort of the orphans now resident there, depending in part upon the insurance money and partly upon the liberality of the people of Kansas City, and of the State at large, for the means of accomplishing this work. And to this end, we the undersigned Trustees, in behalf of the ladies and the orphaned ones under their care, set forth the following appeal to our fellow citizens, believing that the same noble generosity and quick sympathy that prompted them to aid with their thousands the houseless sufferers of the Chicago fire, will not allow them to turn a deaf ear to the suffering of our own people and kindred in similar circumstances:

These orphans and their attendants are now sheltered in a house of three rooms, destitute of provisions, and have but little clothing and furniture left. Even the cooking stove and utensils they are using are borrowed, while at present they cook and eat out of doors, for want of room within. These children vary in age from two years to fifteen years, and are of various nationalities, and from all sections. All, however, are homeless and destitute, and demand the sympathy of all christian people.

Committees will be appointed to solicit aid in money, clothing, provisions, and everything else which the kindness of our friends may incite them to give. Nothing will come amiss, and all will be gratefully received.

Over seven years has this institution been conducted by the noble ladies who are still managing it, and its success has been the result of severe, constant and long continued labor, and our people owe it not less to them than to the orphans themselves, to respond generously to this their *first call upon them for unearned aid*. They need the encouragement of a hearty and warm sympathy in their arduous work at all times, but more particularly now when so great a calamity has befallen them, and in an hour destroyed the work of years.

A small contribution from each citizen, so small as scarcely to be felt, will be an incalculable benefit to this object, and we feel assured that it will not be withheld by any one who will consider for a moment the class of people who are to receive it—POOR, HELPLESS, HOMELESS ORPHANS.

P. S.—Donations in money may be left at the Bank of J. J. Mastin & Co., First National Bank, or any of the city banks, or with Postmaster Case. Donations in clothing, &c., may be sent to Widows' and Orphans' Home.

WM. HOLMES,
L. W. BURRIS,
J. J. MASTIN, TRUSTEES.
WM. BERNARD,
J. LYKINS,

I wrote this appeal & got the trustees to sign it I paid for the printing of this circular out of my own funds - Mrs M E Bingham
P.S. by this appeal we did not receive one dollar -

91

These are examples of articles from Mattie's scrapbook.

"*Kansas City Times*"

—The waif left at the State Line House some days ago and subsequently taken care of by Mr. George Gaston, was returned to the police, Tuesday, for some cause or other, and Deputy Marshal Malloy took it to the Orphan's Home, where it was taken in and christened Rudolph Lykius. Malloy spoke in glowing terms of the "Home" and the generous hearted and benevolent matrons in charge of it.

The little waif is still in the Orphans Home + now called George Bingham Lykius

The Orphan.

A brother writes from Clarksville: "I enclose in my letter ten dollars. Credit me for one year, and send the *Journal* to that orphan girl to whom you so recently referred. If she is receiving the paper, send a copy to some poor minister." This is the second offering which we have received for this purpose.

Acknowledgements.

ORPHANS' HOME, KANSAS CITY, May 22.
Please acknowledge the indebtedness of the Society to the following friends for donations. Will not others send something?

Jas. R. Jackson, Darksville	$5 0
Rev. Wm. M. Bell, miami, (collected from miami church)	20 00
Electia	2 00

T. P. JAUDON, Snp't.

Donors across the state and in western territories where Confederate veterans and Southern sympathizers had moved responded to the women's pleas and sent what they could. A group of Colorado settlers sent a gold brick valued at $500. Small donors dipped into their savings and churches took up collections.

The committee succeeded in raising the funds to establish the Confederate Widows' and Orphans' Home at 32nd and Locust Streets in Kansas City. Mattie lent $1,500 (approximately $35,000 in today's terms) to augment the committee's funds. The committee was then able to purchase 40 acres about two miles south of the city limits, and erect a building costing $5,000 to serve as the home. Initially, four Confederate widows moved in and cared for twelve orphan children.

Mattie's committee continued its energetic and highly skilled fundraising efforts as it tried to sustain the home. The group began publishing, under Mattie's editorship, *The Orphans' Advocate*, a monthly newsletter to publicize the importance of the institution to the community. The clipping on the left is an example of her public relations effort through the newspaper.

With a readership of over 3000 subscribers, the paper continued to tell stories of orphans taken in by the home, of generous benefactors and fundraising events. Still, it was an extreme challenge to keep the orphanage going.

THE ORPHANS' ADVOCATE.

KANSAS CITY, MO. $1.00 PER YEAR.

Devoted to the Interests of the Helpless and Homeless Widows and Orphans of Confederate Soldiers.

Reader, were you a Southern Soldier ? Did you have loved ones in the War ? Or, in any case, do you claim to sympathize with suffering, sorrow, and destitution. In either case, the appeal is to you.

By subscribing for the " ADVOCATE " you will get the worth of your money, bestow a charity, and help advertise the wants and merits of the "Orphans' Home." Please don't make the excuse, that you already have enough reading matter, but remember the cause, and send along a dollar for yourself, and try to raise a club among your neighbors and friends.

The Orphans' Home is now in need ! Who will come to the Rescue ? CAN CONFEDERATE OFFICERS AND SOLDIERS TREAT THE APPEAL WITH DISREGARD ? Money, Clothing, and Provisions of all kinds are wanted.

Address,   MRS. M. A. LYKINS,

Editor Orphans' Advocate, and President Widows' and Orphans' Home Society, Kansas City, Mo.

Kansas City, Mo., August, 1872.   W. A. WASH, AGENT.

PLEASE POST THIS UP.

The Home's benefactors could no longer sustain the home, their resources having been stretched to the limit. The women who had given thousands of dollars and hours of their time to the orphanage asked Missouri Governor Woodson to recommend that the State take charge of the Home, and make it a home to serve orphans from throughout the State. They described the Home's situation, and asked for the legislature's support:

> Though entirely out of debt, it [the home] has no endowment. The necessary expenditures of the institution for superintendence, clothing, tuition, etc., must yet be met by private contributions, rendering necessary continued appeals to private benevolence, which, so constantly repeated, are calculated to exhaust the charity of the liberal, and close their hearts against us. We also feel a depressing consciousness that these contributors have already discharged their whole duty, and that we are doing a wrong in persistently calling upon them to sustain burthens which should be be borne by the State. They have been feeding, clothing and educating your poor, not theirs; and our estimate of your loyalty to duty induces us to believe that, with a knowledge of the fact, you will permit it to exist no longer.
>
> The proceeds of their contributions, exhibited in the real estate of the Home, as already stated, amounted to $40,000, besides the many more thousands which they have given to feed the destitute of the State for a period of more than five years. The annual interest which would accrue from an endowment fund of $50,000 would place the institution in a self-sustaining condition and relieve it from the necessity of humiliating appeals for aid to those who are under no further obligations to render it.

Orphan's Home

KANSAS CITY, MO.

Having failed by a few votes in the Senate to get our Institution placed under the guardian care of the State, we propose trying to sustain it still another year by voluntary donations, hoping and believing that the Legislature will yet agree to receive as a gift the property, and devote it to the welfare of Missouri's homeless, helpless and friendless orphans.

Will those who have aided us before, please once again lend a helping hand? And will those who have never contributed, send along their mite in the cause of humanity? Money, or anything to eat or wear, will be gratefully received.

Address, "Orphan's Home Society, Kansas City, Mo."

APRIL, 1873.

Mrs. M. A. Lykins, *President.*
Mrs. G. C. Bingham,
Mrs. Laura Holmes,
Mrs. Sarah Tyree,
Mrs. S. T. Johnson,
Miss Cinnie Coleman.

W. A. WASH, Agent.

MR. EDITOR: Please publish this for the sake of our Orphan charge.

95

The bill finally passed in March 1874, after failing to pass during two consecutive legislative sessions.

The legislature appropriated $40,000, of which $25,000 was earmarked for the construction of a large, new building (the original building having burned the year before on August 11, 1873).

The map below shows the location of the site, as taken from a newspaper years later when the Little Sisters of the Poor operated their "Home for the Aged" in the former Widows' and Orphans' Home.

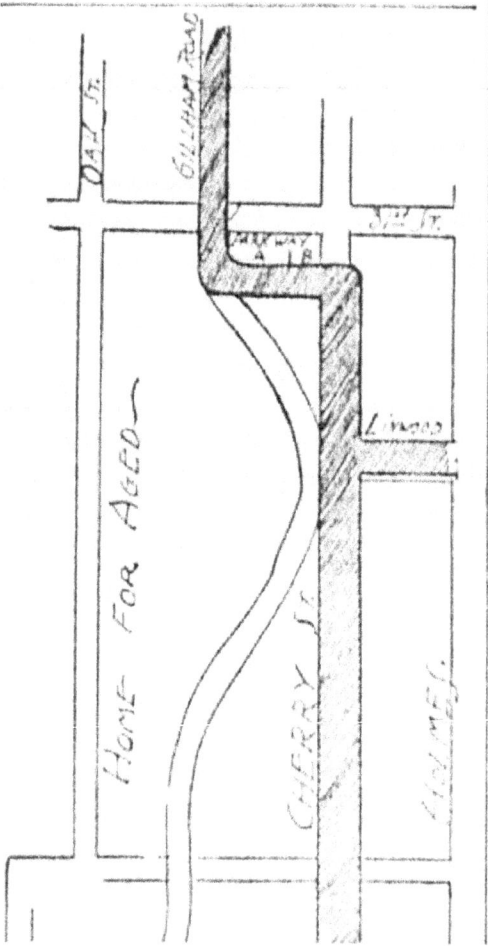

The passage of "Mrs. Lykins' Bill" was celebrated by the Kansas City community and the women savored the success of their tireless campaign. The ceremony for the laying of the cornerstone on June 24, 1874, was conducted by the Masons with great fanfare:

> The city during the morning presented a lively appearance, the streets being thronged with carriages and pedestrians, evidently bent upon attending the celebration. Special arrangements had been made with the street car lines, and every car running to Westport was crowded with passengers. All along the beautiful drive between this city and the Orphans' Home were seen merry loads of pleasure-seekers, some driving, some walking, carry their lunch baskets and dressed in holiday attire.
>
> From Westport came crowds of people flocking to the grounds, seemingly claiming half the honor of the noble institution rearing its walls so near their doors. An extra number of street cars were required to convey these people to the place of festivities.

Gaining state funds for this new building was considered a great coup and a triumph over competing legislative proposals for buildings in St. Louis or at the state's university. The borderland city was in the mood to celebrate the construction of a beautiful three-story Italianate building. The newspaper account hailed the architect, A.J. Kelly, for designing, "the elegant structure now in process of erection [which] will be when completed one of the finest specimens of architecture in the West."

The New Confederate Widows' and Orphans' Home

In 1900, Gillham Road was re-routed around the property of the Little Sisters of the Poor, formerly the Confederate Widows' and Orphans' Home, fronting 31st Street, west of Cherry Street. When, in 1922, the Little Sisters of the Poor were building a new "Home for the Aged" at 53rd and Woodland Avenues, they made preparations to vacate the "ancient structure" they had occupied since 1882.

The jubilation was short-lived. In the very next legislative session, the political mood changed and the legislators failed to provide further funds to the orphanage. Theodore Case, Mattie's former son-in-law and lifelong friend, wrote that with the construction of the new industrial home for orphans statewide and state funding, the institution should have been well-supported and established. Instead, he reported regretfully:

98

Owing to the jealousy of other localities, and perhaps some religious and political opposition, the Legislature failed to make further provision for its support and the property returned to the original society. Having no sure means of support, the society attempted to sustain the Home in connection with a female seminary; but this not proving satisfactory, the whole project was abandoned. It was much to the disgrace of the State of Missouri that the Legislature failed to provide for a benevolent institution of this kind, which they had founded, and which would have been of so much public benefit.

THE JOURNAL.

FRIDAY, MARCH 13, 1874.

THE ORPHAN'S HOME.

MRS. LYKINS has been rewarded for her long, patient and persistent efforts to establish an orphans' home at Kansas City, to be endowed and supported by the state. We give her the chief place, and while we do not forget other and many kind friends who aided, yet they will all, we know, generously second our declaration that to her belongs the chief honor of this good work. It will be a material advantage to our city, but that consideration is small, compared to the unselfish devotion with which Mrs. LYKINS has labored for the success she has so worthily won. The home will be a monument to her memory long after she has gone from us, and for years in the future, the orphans provided for will hold her memory in veneration and affection.

Years of effort and sacrifice by Mattie, the women and trustees of the home and its many benefactors had now ended in this bitter disappointment.

Not to be undone, Mattie attempted to keep the de-funded Widows' and Orphans' home afloat by establishing an academy for girls, The Lykins Institute, at the site of the former orphanage where she continued to live.

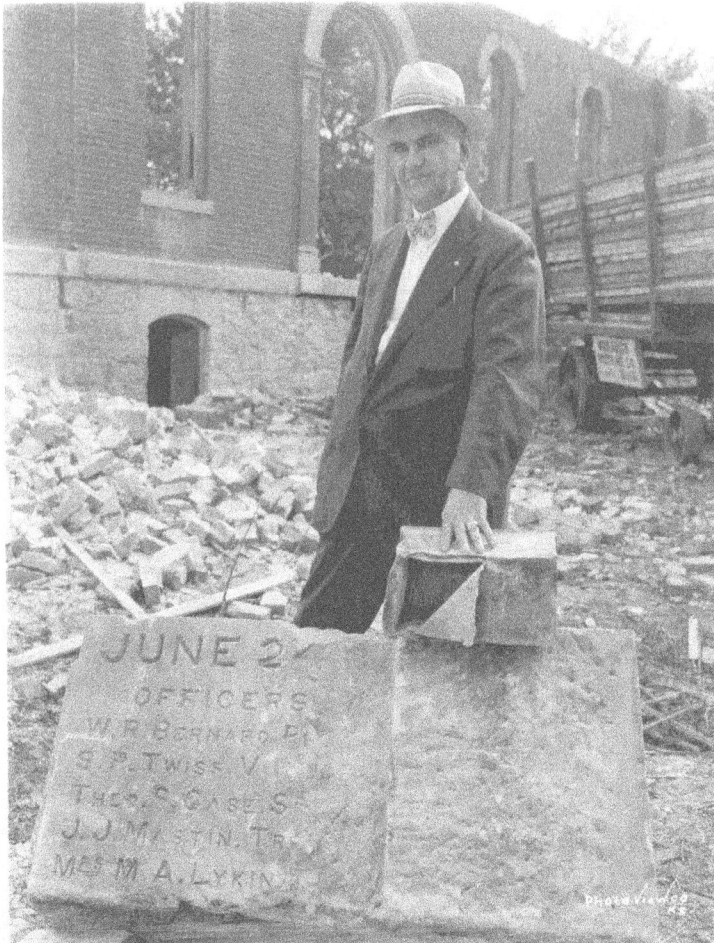

Ben Jaudon, Director of Finance for Kansas City, Missouri, standing behind the cornerstone and rubble from the demolished Confederate Widows' and Orphans' Home, which had been used by the Little Sisters of the Poor from 1882-1922.

Engraved on the cornerstone dated June 24, 1874, are officers of the original Home: W. R. Bernard, President; S. P. Twiss, Vice President; Theodore S. Case, Secretary; J. J. Martin, Treasurer; and Mrs. M. A. Lykins, Superintendent. The back side contained the names: A. J. Kelly, architect; and J. M. Jackson, contractor.

Soon thereafter, on August 15, 1876, Mattie's husband, Johnston Lykins, died in financial ruin in a room on the third floor of the The Lykins Institute.

Mattie constructed a new life following the bankruptcy and death of her husband. She sold the beautiful mansion she and Johnston had built—probably because she had to—and continued to live at The Lykins Institute.

Evolution and Demise of the Lykins Mansion

The Lykins mansion was sold to John Mastin in 1876. Several families occupied the house in intervening years. Subsequent owners were Major R. S. Henning; L. T. Moore (of Bullene, Moore & Emery . . . later Emery, Bird, Thayer department store); and, Charles D. Hasbrook.

From at least 1888, Mrs. R. L. Upton conducted a school for girls there. In mid-September 1889, George W. Strope contracted with William A. Bovard, Sr., to move the mansion across the street from the southeast corner to the southwest corner of 12th and Washington Streets. "Kansas City's first mansion" was threatened with destruction at that time when proposed construction of the Washington Hotel was slated for the southeast corner. [The Washington Hotel was subsequently built on the southeast corner; it burned on April 22, 1953, and was razed in October. Today, that site—the *original* location of the Lykins mansion—is the headquarters for the Kansas City Southern Railway Company.]

After its relocation to the southwest corner, Upton continued her school there for a time. At some point, a third, top- story was added to the former Lykins mansion, having no architectural relationship to the classic southern lines of the original 2-story mansion. Historic images suggest that a ground-floor was also added at the time of its relocation, making the building a 4-story structure.

In 1891, Miss Brann and Miss Barstow moved their "Barstow School" from a Broadway location to the former Lykins mansion [subsequently the Barstow School expanded and moved to quarters at Westport and Baltimore Avenues, before moving to a newer school development on 15th Street, between Cherry and Oak Streets].

By 1923, it was being operated as the Roslin Hotel (and may have also been the Mondamin Hotel at some point). The next year or two, however, just south of it, on ground once a lawn, an apartment hotel was to be built. A 1942 newspaper article claimed it had been a hotel for 44 years (or, 1898).

Views of the Lykins mansion. Opposite bottom: original Southern mansion with east-facing, two-story, covered porticos; top: after relocation with added top <u>and</u> street-level floors for adaptive reuse into a commercial structure. Above: June 27, 1989, shows the east-facing, Washington Street façade—*without* the added top-story—the original, two-story mansion discernable in the distinctive, double-side-lighted entryways (formerly, the covered porticos).

In 1989, the Historic Kansas City Foundation, a non-profit corporation dedicated to the restoration and preservationof Kansas City's historic buildings and early neighborhoods, had an option-to-buy contract with the then owner of the former Lykins mansion. The option gave them the right to purchase the house for $16 a square foot. Susan Cline-Cordonier, HKCF executive director at that time, said, "We need about a half million to purchase and stabilize it for redevelopment—do a simple board-up to protect it from the elements."

The effort needed to be accomplished before midnight on September 29, 1989, the hour and day for expiration of HKCF's option.

Clearly, local historic preservation efforts were unsuccessful. The site today is a parking lot for surrounding businesses.

Mattie and George Caleb Bingham

Mattie and George Caleb Bingham, both having recently lost their spouses, began to spend time together. Her friendship with the renowned painter and Missouri politician deepened into a serious romantic relationship. One of Bingham's self-portraits, painted in 1877, is thought to have been painted for Mattie during their courtship. Alberta Wilson Constant, a Bingham biographer, noted the differences between the self-portrait Bingham painted and a photograph taken of him two years later, observing that Bingham emphasized a "hidden smile in his eyes" to take the viewer's attention away from the lines on his face and to look more fetchingly youthful.

George Caleb Bingham
Self-Portrait, ca. 1877

Mattie found herself again at the center of controversy. She gradually influenced Bingham to affiliate with Unitarianism, which would have been considered a radical departure from conventional faith. But what caused Kansas City tongues to wag the most was that Bingham moved in with Mattie before their marriage.

A further cause for scandal was that one of her avowed enemies, a Mr. Piper, was the brother-in-law of Bingham's deceased wife. Piper had earlier opposed Mattie's plan for establishing the orphanage. In a public exchange, Mattie had thoroughly outdone him and he was determined to get revenge. When Mattie and Bingham began to live together, Piper saw an opportunity. He and his wife turned Bingham's sixteen-year-old son, Rollins, against Mattie, filling the boy's imagination with visions of Mattie robbing him of his father's wealth and legacy. Bingham's best friend stepped in and told the boy he was in danger of having his father cut off his allowance, a move which abruptly quieted the teenager who had been trumpeting his displeasure with Mattie throughout the city.

Soon afterward, Mattie and Bingham were married at the Lykins Institute on June 18, 1878. A guest at the wedding described the festive decorations for the event:

From the centre of the back parlor . . . was a magnificent wedding bell . . . constructed of the sombre bloom of the smoke tree, festooned with heliotrope and honeysuckle. . . . The pair stood there, he the successful artist whose well-known paintbrush has painted pictures that shall live forever, and she, an acknowledged equal in taste, aesthetic culture

Portrait of an Unknown Woman ("Mrs. General Bingham," a missing painting by George Caleb Bingham?)

105

and expressive sensibility, the scene was not joyous but impressive. The congratulations were prompt and hearty, all the guests but one being younger than the newly married couple.... A most bountiful breakfast was partaken by the guests–a royal feast–its real and true description impossible.

Bingham's health improved for a short time, and he was very happy with Mattie, telling his friend James Rollins "that he hoped to live long enough so 'that I may be able in some measure, to

compensate her for the unselfish love which exhibits itself in her every act relating to myself.'"

Their marital happiness was short-lived. In a little over a year, George Caleb Bingham died in July 1879. Mattie arranged for his burial in the plot next to Johnston Lykins at Union Cemetery.

She contacted John Alan Campbell, a sculptor and the husband of her niece, Lizzie Owen Campbell. He agreed to design the tombstone and sculpt a medallion of Bingham's bust as its central feature.[13] Mattie had the 11-foot monument erected for

Bingham on which was inscribed, *"Eminently gifted, almost unaided he won such distinction in his profession that he is known as the Missouri artist."*

Mattie did what she could to keep Bingham's legacy as an artist alive by advertising engravings and canvases from Bingham's studio. For several years, she exhibited the collection she had inherited from him at the Brunswick Hotel in Kansas City.

Despite her efforts, Bingham's painting was forgotten. When his paintings were sold at auction in 1893, they brought very little money, some selling for as little as $35.00. A Bingham biographer, Paul Nagel, wrote that Bingham's work was not noticed again by critics until the 1930s, long after he and his wife, Mrs. General Bingham, were alive to bask in the recognition that he was, indeed, an important American artist.

In the years following Bingham's death, Mattie continued to work for the well-being of women and children. In 1884, Mattie served on the Board of Managers for the Kansas City Exchange for Women's Work, serving more than once as President of the organization.[14] This organization, also known as The Women's Exchange, provided a market outlet for products made by women. Large cities across the nation established these organizations to assist women in independently providing a living for themselves and their children. Recognizing that many women had excellent skills, but no way to use them in the marketplace, the Kansas City Women's Exchange established a sales room and popular luncheon room at Ninth and Main. There the needlework of the women was displayed and sold and many city residents benefitted from their home cooking. The organization was conceptually a forerunner of contemporary projects which give home-bound, place-bound women in third world countries opportunities to use their skills to sustain their families and to learn to manage their own money.

When Mattie married Bingham, she unwittingly inherited his family problems along with his estate. George Bingham's brother, Matthias, owned large amounts of property in Texas, and at the time of Matthias' death, his heirs, including George, disputed the division of the property. Mattie was drawn into the issue by virtue of having inherited her husband's estate.

In addition, she became the guardian of Bingham's son, Rollins. Her charge lived with her at the Lykins Institute and studied law. Mattie hoped that Rollins' legal background would result in his being able to settle the land dispute and manage her other business and legal affairs as well.

In the meantime, former donors to the Confederate Widows' and Orphans' Home were displeased when trustees voted to give the home's remaining assets to Mattie to compensate her for her years of service as president and, later, supervisor of the home (1866-1880). They also filed a lawsuit, which was dismissed years later because the plaintiffs were determined to not have legal standing in the case.

The problems coming from Rollins' handling of the legal matters came to a head when Cornelia Lykins, wife of Mattie's stepson, W. H. R. Lykins, asked Mattie why a deed held in trust in Mattie's estate had been signed over as security for a loan.[15] Mattie was astounded! She had not authorized this action at all, and began to realize that Rollins had been forging her name on financial and real estate documents. Even as she moved to protect herself, she tried to shield her step-son to whom she had become close. Six weeks before her death, trying to cover for Rollins, she proclaimed to creditors that he had not committed forgery.

Death of a Missouri Star

Unfortunately, Mattie did not live long enough either to untangle her legal and financial affairs, or to protect Rollins. On September 20, 1890, she died of cancer shortly after her discovery of the forgery, having undergone stomach surgery and developed complications leading to her death.

Mattie died in her rooms at the Washington Hotel which had been built on the original site of her and Johnston Lykins' spacious home. The home in which she had spent the majority of her years in

Kansas City had been moved to a lot across the street after its sale years earlier. The *Kansas City Star* on September 22 reported:

The Funeral of Mrs. Bingham

The funeral services of Mrs. M. A. Bingham took place at 4'oclock yesterday afternoon at All Souls church, the Rev. Dr. [--?--] Roberts delivered the sermon. The choir, at the closing, rendered Cardinal Newman's "Lead, Kindly Light." Interment was in Union Cemetery.

Because of the notoriety caused by Rollins' forgery and his abrupt departure from the city, Mattie's Last Will and Testament was printed in the newspaper in its entirety. In the Will she gave Rollins her library and some of his father's paintings; and, some cash to her nephew Alphonse Hughes, and two nieces, Lizzie Owen Campbell, and Laura Owen Mills.[16]

The proceeds of the sale of her collection of Bingham paintings were to go to an Ex-Confederate Home in Higginsville, Missouri.

At the end of her life, she continued to look out for those whose lives were broken by the Civil War. The estate, which was not settled for several more years, included a number of Bingham paintings. Her portrait, "Mrs. General Bingham," probably among those, was tied up in the complicated disputes surrounding the

settlement. It is believed to have been among those family portraits sold at auction in 1893 to settle the estate, although Mattie had, at some point, willed it to her niece, Lizzie Campbell. This Bingham portrait may have recently been re-discovered, as noted in the Illustrations section at the end of the book (see image caption "105. 'Mrs. General Bingham'"). Should this be authenticated as Mattie, it would match Bingham's self-portrait with an equally 'romantic' brush stroke; both Bingham and Mattie were quite a bit older than as painted.

The mystery of what had happened to Rollins Bingham was not solved until he turned himself in to law officers in Dallas, Texas, in 1902. His health was ruined and he was destitute. He justified his forgery of Mattie's documents by saying that he was trying to protect Mattie by using her money to garner a windfall of wealth through investment.[17] Some Missouri newspaper accounts of the time offered a different explanation, reporting that people who knew him in Kansas City remembered him as a "hail-fellow-well-met" young man who was fond of lavish living and chasing women. When he was voluntarily removed to Missouri to face charges, he was acquitted because the men whose names were forged on documents and had filed charges (one of them Alphonse Hughes, Mattie's nephew) were no longer alive.[18] Other witnesses, out of respect for his father or pity for Rollins, declined to come forward. Rollins became a journalist in Kansas City and, his health destroyed, died of pneumonia in 1910 at the age of 47.

Even in death, Mattie caused comment by having arranged to be buried between the two eminent husbands with a small stone marking her grave. A more conventional practice was to bury spouses of a first marriage together. Mattie chose to rest beside both husbands with the monument she placed for Bingham dwarfing both hers and Johnston's.

Mattie's unconventional choices, outspoken ways, and controversial stances did not obscure the substance of her character. Her resilience carried her through losses, betrayal and criticism.

Through it all, refusing to be crushed or silenced, she prevailed. In a newspaper article written years after her death:

> The contemporaries of Mrs. Lykins pronounced her the biggest-hearted and broadest-minded of all the pioneer women of Kansas City. She was one of the most remarkable characters that ever lived in this community. With a strong mind, strengthened by a broad and liberal education, a commanding presence, manners of the most cultivated society, a powerful intellect and a tenacious will, she devoted her life to the welfare and happiness of the helpless and destitute. She was the foremost woman in every charitable and public work of early Kansas City. With success she was never satisfied and in defeat, she never surrendered.[19]

She was an articulate, bright and compassionate woman who would not be constrained by the roles and opinions commonly held in her time. As George Caleb Bingham said of her, *"I think I can safely say in the highest sense of the term, she is no ordinary woman."*

Mattie did not know—or care to know—how to walk a conventional path . . . it would never have occurred to her.

[1] Jordan Dodd, "Missouri Marriages to 1850," database, Ancestry.com (http://www.ancestry.com/search : accessed November 29, 2010), entry for Thomas J. Hughes and Rebecca Livingston.

[2] Jacqueline Hogan Williams, *Lafayette, Missouri Abstract of Wills and Administrations, 1821-1850* (Warrensburg, Missouri: Jacqueline Hogan Williams, 1968),48.

[3] J.P. Munro-Fraser, *History of Contra Costa, California: including its geography, geology topography, climatology and description; together with a record of the Mexican grants...also, incidents of pioneer life; and biographical sketches of early and prominent settlers and representative men.* (San Francisco: W.A. Slocum & Co., 1882), 223.

[4] *History of Marion County, Missouri: written and compiled from the most authentic official and private sources: including a history of its townships, towns, and villages, together with a condensed history of Missouri, the city of St. Louis, a reliable and detailed history of Marion County, its pioneer record, war history, resources, biographical sketches and portraits of prominent citizens: general and local statistics of great value, and a large amount of legal and miscellaneous matter, incidents and reminiscences, grave, tragic and humorous.* 1884 reprint. (La Crosse, Wis: Brookhaven Press, 2000*)*, 365.

[5] House Committee of Claims, "Kansas Claims," p.800, Claim No. 187 (Stephen J. Livingston), 22 Apr 1859, list of losses.

[6] *Mattie Lykins Scrapbook,* microfilm in Dr. Johnston Lykins (1800-1876) and Martha Lykins Bingham (1824-1890) Collection, KC-0294; Native Sons of Greater Kansas City Archives, State Historical Society of Missouri Research Center-Kansas City, Kansas City, Missouri.

[7] Eugene Ferguson to [unnamed] niece, letter, nd, typed transcript, Lykins file; Union Cemetery Historical Society, Kansas City, Missouri.

[8] Undated, unattributed newspaper article in the Jackson County (Mo.) Historical Society Archives Vertical Subject File.

[9] Undated, unattributed newspaper article in the Jackson County (Mo.) Historical Society Archives Vertical Subject File.

[10] Martin Rice. *Rural Rhymes, and Talks and Tales of Olden Times.* (Lone Jack, Mo.: Martin Rice, 1893).

[11] McCullough, David. *Truman.*(New York: Simon & Schuster Paperbacks, 1992), 32.

[12] *Case files of applications from former Confederates for Presidential pardons (Amnesty papers) 1865-1867,* Microfilm publication M1003, roll 36 (Washington, D.C., National Archives and Records Service, 1977), roll 36, Mattie Lykins to President Andrew Johnson, letter, 11 June 1866, as transcribed by Carolyn M. Bartels, compiler, *Amnesty in Missouri* (Shawnee Mission, Kansas: C.M. Bartels, 2990, np, and reprinted in *Kansas City Genealogist,* 35 (Fall 1994): 86-87.

[13] Jean Hamilton Tyree, "Mr. Bingham's Tombstone," *Missouri Historical Review,* Columbia, Missouri: The State Historical Society of Missouri, ed. Richard S. Brownlee, Volume 1, no. 1, July 1979, 429.

[14] "Mrs. M.A. Bingham Is Dead. Quietly, Peacefully A Remarkable Woman Passes Away," *Kansas City* (Mo.) *Times*, 21 Sept. 1890, p. 1, c. 6.

[15] "Bingham Gone. The Lawyer Leaves in Disgrace. His Stepmother's Name Forged Before Her Death." *The Kansas City* (Mo.) *Times*, 4 Nov. 1890.

[16] "Mrs. Bingham's Will. Requests of Cash to Various Relatives—Her Books and Paintings," *The Kansas City* (Mo.) *Times,* 23 Sept. 1890.

[17] "Prodigal's Story. James Rollins Bingham's Letter to Prosecuting Attorney at Kansas City," *Fort Worth* (Tx.) *Morning Register*, 5 Feb 1902.

[18] "Rollins Bingham is Free.The Charge of Forgery Dismissed by the Prosecution Today." *The Kansas City* (Mo.) *Star, 26* May 1902.

[19] "Mystery in an Opened Corner Stone," undated clipping from unidentified newspaper; Kansas History Clippings, v. 6, p. 314; Kansas State Historical Society, Topeka, Kansas.

CHAPTER 5

Ancestral Connections

Mattie's Ancestral Claims

Martha Ann "Mattie" (Livingston) Lykins Bingham fervently believed that she was a direct lineal descendant of **Philip Livingston**, signer of the Declaration of Independence. Further, she proudly claimed that she and **General Stonewall Jackson** of the Confederate Army were second cousins. These claims have been frequently repeated in biographical sketches of her life and even in her obituary. Genealogical researchers, however, have not been successful in finding the links between her family and those of either Philip Livingston or Stonewall Jackson.

How could she or, alternatively, genealogical researchers be so mistaken? Two possibilities come to mind:

1. She fell victim to a well-known genealogical error, popularly known as **"The Name's the Same."** For example, a person might have a father named "Captain Stephen Livingston" and then find out that one of Philip Livingston's descendants living in New York also has the name **"Captain Stephen Livingston."** Then she or whoever told her of this relationship assume that they are the same person when, in fact, they are not. Certainly knowing about her ancestral roots was highly dependent on oral tradition. Neither she

nor the genealogists of her era had access to the national databases and research capabilities at the fingertips of today's genealogists. Most genealogical information was passed down through the family by way of family Bibles or the historical memories of family members.

In Mattie's case, she would have been particularly reliant on the knowledge and memories of one or both of her grandmothers, **Sarah Cathell Livingston and Martha Maddera Jackson.** (A death date is not known for either of them and Mattie only mentioned that she spent her childhood with her grandmother and did not specify which one.) Both of Mattie's parents died before she was four years old, at which time Mattie went to live with one of her grandmothers. Both grandmothers appear to have died before 1836. Sarah's paternal grandfather, **James Livingston,** had also been long dead.

2.   Another possibility is that the family connections Mattie claimed were valid, but that genealogists have not figured out what the linkages are. Most genealogical researchers try to trace the **Stonewall Jackson** claim by looking at Mattie's mother, Martha Jackson, and they do not find a connection. John C. Jackson was thought by Ermine Jett Darnell to be connected to Stonewall Jackson's family; he lived near Francis Jackson; in fact, John C. Jackson testified to support Francis Jackson's Revolutionary War pension that he and Francis Jackson had known each other for many years, both in Virginia and in Kentucky. Another direction to explore is the surname "Cathell", Sarah Livingston's surname, which is prevalent in West Virginia where Stonewall Jackson grew up.

Who is Mattie's Paternal Grandfather?

Researchers have been perplexed about the identity of Mattie's paternal grandfather. Her Grandmother Sarah's badly transcribed signature on a marriage record for her daughter has resulted in the name "Sereneye Livingston" with researchers scrambling to find out if such a name existed and scouring census records to find him. Ermine Jett Darnell (*The Forks of Elkhorn Church*, 1947) reported that Sarah Livingston lived in the vicinity of the church (northern Woodford County, near the Franklin County line) and had three known children, Stephen (Mattie's father), Ellen and Elizabeth. The 1810 census of Woodford County slaveholders listed Sarah Livingston with hash marks indicating that she had three persons under 25 in the household. There seemed to be no sign of a Livingston who could be Stephen's father anywhere in the county, and Mattie's grandfather could not be accounted for in surrounding counties.

By using indirect evidence tucked between the various censuses a case can be made that a Livingston man from Maryland was Sarah's husband. Sarah's daughter Ellender Victoria (Livingston) Edrington declared in both the 1850 and 1860 censuses that she was born in Maryland around 1795. An examination of early Kentucky histories and land records revealed a "Maryland presence" among early Kentucky settlers. William Todd Livingston's settlement in the Virginia wilderness which became Fincastle County Kentucky is a frequently cited example because of the attack of Chief Benge on the settlement and the tomahawking of Livingston's wife. None of William Todd Livingston's children or those of his sons, however, appear to fit the bill. Other surnames suggest that people related to the Maryland Livingstons by marriage also lived in or near Woodford County: Levi Todd, the tax assessor for the county, and "Innis (Ennis) Bottoms," the location of the Cook settlement in 1792. Sarah Livingston's daughter, Elizabeth, married Hosea Cook,

Jr., the son of the Hosea Cook killed in the massacre at Cook's Station.

Lucile Barco Coone in *The Livingstons of Virginia* (1990) identified William Todd Livingston as the brother of George Livingston Senior, a merchant. George Livingston Sr.'s wife, Sarah Horsey Livingston, separated from her husband, taking her children with her to her parents' home in Worcester County. When Sarah Horsey Livingston's will was probated in 1793, James Livingston was listed as one of her sons. James Livingston (believed by some researchers to be George and Sarah Horsey Livingston's son) married Sarah Cathell in 1787. (There may, however, have been two or more James Livingstons in Maryland during the latter part of the eighteenth century.) This James Livingston had three sons and three daughters.

In an article by Robert R. Shriver, "Livingstons of the Lower Eastern Shore of Maryland as known to the middle of the 1800s" (in *Potpourri from our Files: Family Records of the Lower Eastern Shore,* Vol 3, Spring, 1997 published by DelMarva Genealogical Society, Salisbury, MD), the birth dates for the children are consistent with years of birth reported by Ellen(der) (Livingston) Edrington and Elizabeth (Livingston) Cook in the 1850 census. Three of the names provided in the list match those known to be children of Sarah Livingston in Woodford County, Kentucky: Stephen, Ellen, and Elizabeth. Shriver's information about James and Sarah (Cathell) Livingston's family was recorded on blank leaves in books by their son, Joshua Livingston.

Woodford County tax lists from between 1806 and 1812 support the notion that a James Livingston is Sarah Livingston's husband and Stephen's father. James Livingston did not own land upon which he paid taxes in Woodford County, but he did own water course rights on Glenn Creek, suggesting that he made his living using the water course, perhaps as a whiskey distiller or grist miller. He was assessed for taxes in 1806 and 1808 (in 1807 and 1809 he may have been assessed along a water course in another county). By 1810, the year Sarah was listed as a head of household and slaveholder, Stephen Livingston paid water course taxes on Glenn Creek. These two facts suggest that James Livingston was dead by 1810 and that Stephen continued with his business.

When Sarah Livingston died, she was, according to Ermine Jett Darnell, buried on "the Old Walcott farm" south of Frankfort. This farmland and the Walcott community lay between South Frankfort on the north and Glenn Creek on the south. Glenn Creek flows through southeastern Franklin County, near Frankfort, and northwestern Woodford County, the county in which James Livingston paid taxes. It is reasonable to think that Sarah Livingston was buried near her husband. A 1925 topographic map shows an enlarged cemetery situated on this land.

An 1835 Frankfort mansion, easily a prototype for the Lykins mansion

Franklin County Courthouse which dates from 1835, approximately the time two of Mattie's grandparents died. She would have been assigned to a guardian here, and six years later, would have received an inheritance settlement here. This building survives today (2011); but, its fate may be uncertain.

Ancestors of Martha Ann "Mattie" (Livingston) Lykins Bingham

First Generation

1. Martha Ann "Mattie" Livingston, daughter of **Stephen Livingston** and **Martha Jackson**, was born in January 1824 near Frankfort, Franklin County, Kentucky,[1] died on 20 September 1890 in Kansas City, Jackson County, Missouri,[2] and was buried on 21 September 1890 in Union Cemetery, Kansas City, Jackson County, Missouri.[3]

Martha married **Johnston Lykins**, son of **David L. Lykins** and **Jemima Willis**, on 12 October 1851 in Lexington, Lafayette County, Missouri.[4]

Martha next married **George Caleb Bingham**, son of **Henry Vest Bingham** and **Maria Christiana Amend**, on 18 June 1878 in Kansas City, Jackson County, Missouri.[5]

Second Generation (Parents)

2. Stephen Livingston, son of **James Livingston** and **Sarah Cathell**, was born on 19 June 1788 in Worcester County, Maryland,[6] died about 1828 in Frankfort, Franklin, Kentucky,[7] and was buried in South Frankfort, Franklin County, Kentucky.[8]

Stephen married **Martha Jackson** on 12 November 1812 in Woodford County, Kentucky.[9]

Children from this marriage were:

> i. **Elizabeth Livingston** was born about 1815 in Kentucky[10] and died about 1883 in Shelbyville, Shelby County, Kentucky.[11]
>
> ii. **William J. Livingston** was born in 1819 in Kentucky[12] and died on 19 August 1864 in St. Louis, Missouri.[13]
>
> iii. **John Henry Livingston** was born about 1821 in Kentucky.[14]
>
> iv. **Rebecca Livingston** was born before 1824 in Kentucky.[15]

1   v.   **Martha Ann Livingston**
       vi.   **Stephen J. Livingston** was born in 1825 in Frankfort, Kentucky[16] and died before 1880 in Monmouth Township, Shawnee, Kansas.[17]

3. Martha "Patsey" Jackson, daughter of **Francis Jackson** and **Martha Maddera,** was born on 18 April 1795 in Woodford County, Kentucky,[18] died between 1825 and 1828 in Kentucky,[19] and was buried in South Frankfort, Franklin, Kentucky.[20]

Martha married **Stephen Livingston** on 12 November 1812 in Woodford County, Kentucky.[21]

Third Generation (Grandparents)

4. James Livingston, son of **George Livingston Sr.** and **Sarah Horsey,** was born on 30 September1763 in Somerset County, Maryland,[22] and died about 1808 in Woodford County, Kentucky.[23]

James married **Sarah Cathell** on 13 September 1787.[24]

Children from this marriage were:

       i.   **Nancy Livingston** was born on 26 September1786 in Worcester County, Maryland.[25]
2   ii.   **Stephen Livingston**
       iii.   **Joshua C. Livingston** was born on 25 Dec 1789 in Worcester County, Maryland.[26]
       v.   **Ellender "Nellie" Victoria Livingston** was born about 1795 in Maryland[27] and died after 1860 in Columbus, Hickman County, Kentucky.[28]
       iv.   **Elizabeth "Betsy" Livingston** was born about 1796 in Worcester County, Maryland[29] and died after 1860 in Columbus, Hickman, Kentucky.[30]

5. Sarah Cathell, was born on 28 Nov 1762[31] and died about 1838 in Frankfort, Franklin, Kentucky.[32]

Sarah married **James Livingston** on 13 September 1787.[33]

6. Francis Jackson, son of **Francis Jackson** and **Sarah Burton**, was born in August 1757 in Amelia County, Virginia,[34] and died about March 1835 in Woodford County, Kentucky.[35]

Francis married **Martha Maddera** on 10 February 1778 in Amelia County, Virginia.[36]

The children from this marriage were:

	i.	**Madra Jackson** was born on 23 March 1779 in Amelia County, Virginia,[37] and died after 1850 in Jefferson County, Kentucky[38]
	ii.	**John Alpin Jackson** was born on 7 January 1781 in Amelia County, Virginia.[39]
	iii.	**Joshua Jackson** was born on 12 April 1782 in Amelia County, Virginia.[40]
	iv.	**Rebecca Jackson** was born on 30 January 1784 in Amelia County, Virginia.[41]
	v.	**Francis Jackson** was born on 4 December 1785 in Amelia County, Virginia.[42]
	vi.	**Nancy Jackson** was born on 27 September 1789 in Woodford County, Kentucky.[43]
	vii.	**Susanna Jackson** was born on 15 April 1793 in Woodford County, Kentucky.[44]
3	viii.	**Martha Jackson**[45]
	ix.	**Eliza Jackson** was born on 2 June 1796 in Woodford County, Kentucky.[46]
	x.	**Lewis Jackson** was born on 14 May 1797 in Woodford County, Kentucky.[47]
	xi.	**Micajah Jackson** was born on 27 January 1801 in Woodford County, Kentucky.[48]

7. Martha Maddera, daughter of **John Maddera** and **Elizabeth --?--**, was born before 1761.[49]

Martha married **Francis Jackson** on 10 February 1778 in Amelia County, Virginia.[50]

---

[1] C. R. Barnes, editor, *The Commonwealth of Missouri: A Centennial Record* (Saint Louis: Bryan, Brand & Company, 1877), 770.

[2] "Missouri Birth and Death Records Database, Pre-1910," database, Missouri State Archives, *Missouri Digital Heritage* (http://www.sos.mo.gov.archives/resources/birthdeath/ : accessed 27 Nov 2010), death of Bingham, Martha A.

[3] Union Cemetery Historical Society, *Tombstone Inscriptions* (Kansas City: Union Cemetery Historical Society, 1986), 8.

[4] Barnes, *The Commonwealth of Missouri*, 770.

[5] Paul C. Nagel, *George Caleb Bingham: Missouri's Famed Painter and Forgotten Politician* (Columbia, Missouri: University of Missouri Press, 2005), 146.

[6] Linda Livingston Moore, Descendants of George Livingston Livingston; outline descendants chart, *Livingston Family* (www.hto-livingston.com : accessed 4 June 2011), Stephen Livingston and Sara Cathell family group.

[7] Franklin County, Kentucky, Inventory and Sales Book A: 92-93, Stephen Livingston Inventory, 30 August 1828; Legal Records Department, County Clerk's Office, Frankfort, Kentucky. No record of his death date survives. The date of his inventory makes it likely that he died in August 1828.

[8] Nettie Henry Glenn, *Early Frankfort Kentucky, 1786-1861* (Kentucky?: N. H. Glenn, 1986), 169. If he was living with his mother and his children in 1828 when he died, he likely would have been buried in the burial ground at the corner of Bridge and Second streets in South Frankfort, only three short blocks from the house on lot 13 on the corner of Second and Shelby streets.

[9] Dona Adams Wilson, compiler, *Marriage Bonds and Consents, Woodford County, Kentucky, 1789-1830* (Versailles, Kentucky: Woodford County Historical Society, 1998), 1: np. The collection is made up entirely of photocopies of original documents from the archive of the courthouse. The photocopies are arranged alphabetically by name of groom within a series of ring binders. The two documents for Stephen Livingston are his bond and the minister's return of the marriage.

[10] Kentucky Department for Libraries and Archives, "Kentucky Birth Records 1852-1910," database, *Ancestry.com* (http://search.ancestry.com/ : accessed 10 Dec 2010), birth of Elizabeth Owen.

[11] Charlotte Ryder DAR Application, "Descendants Database Search," database, *DAR Genealogical Research Databases* (http://services.dar.org/public/dar research-descendants : accessed 9 Dec 2010), death of Elizabeth Livingston Owen.

[12] 1850 U.S. census, District no. 2, Shelby County, Kentucky, p. 374 (stamped), dwelling 480, family 494; digital image, *Ancestry.com* (http://www.ancestry.com/ : accessed 8 September 2010); citing National Archives and Records Administration microfilm M432, roll 218. See also Ermina Jett Darnell, *Forks of Elkhorn Church with Genealogies of Early Members* (Louisville, Kentucky: Standard Printing, 1946), 190.

[13] "Missouri's Union Provost Marshal Records, 1861-1866," database, report of H. H. Williams to Col. Sanderson reporting hanging of William Jackson Livingston in Saint Louis, 19 August 1864; Missouri State Archives, *Missouri Digital Heritage* (http://www.sos.mo.gov/archives/provost/ : accessed 25 August 2010).

[14] 1860 U.S. census, Township No. 1, Contra Costa County, California, p. 55, dwelling 435, family 435, John H. Livingston; digital image, *Ancestry.com* (http://www.ancestry.com/ : accessed 8 September 2010); citing National Archives and Records Administration microfilm M653, roll 57. John H. Livingston was the census enumerator for this township.

[15] 1850 U.S. census, District no. 1, Nicholas County, Kentucky, p. 478 (stamped), dwelling 440, family 442, Rebecca Hughes; digital image, *Ancestry.com* (http://www.ancestry.com/ : accessed 8 September 2010); citing National Archives and Records Administration microfilm M432, roll 215.

[16] 1850 U.S. census, District no. 1, Franklin County, Kentucky, p. 20 (stamped), dwelling and family 261, Stephen J. Livingston; digital image, *Ancestry.com* (http://www.ancestry.com/ :

accessed 8 September 2010); citing National Archives and Records Administration microfilm M432, roll 200.

[17] 1880 U.S. census, Monmouth, Shawnee County, Kansas, ED 16, p. 5, dwelling and family 34, Lizzie Livingston [widow]; digital image, *Ancestry.com* (http://www.ancestry.com/ : accessed 8 September 2010); citing National Archives and Records Administration microfilm T9, roll 397.

[18] Births of the Children of Francis Jackson, Jackson Family Bible, family pages only; typescript, Filson Historical Society, Louisville, Kentucky; retyped copy in Jackson folder, Surname Files, Martin F. Schmidt Research Library, Thomas D. Clark Center for Kentucky History, Kentucky Historical Society, Frankfort, Kentucky. The Bible was originally owned by Sabina Schacelford Jackson Cox, daughter of Francis Jackson's oldest son, Maddra, and was in the possession of Lyman Cox, Owensburg, Kentucky, as of 1936.

[19] *The History of Jackson County, Missouri* (Kansas City, Missouri: Union Historical Company, 1881), 741. Daughter Martha said that she'd lost both of her parents by the time she was four years old. Thus, her mother died sometime between the birth of Martha's youngest sibling in 1825 and 1828 when she turned four years old.

[20] Glenn, *Early Frankfort Kentucky, 1786-186*, 169. If Stephen and Martha were living on lot 13 in South Frankfort when Martha died, she likely would have been buried in the burial ground at the corner of Bridge and Second streets in South Frankfort, only three short blocks from the house.

[21] Wilson, *Marriage Bonds and Consents, Woodford County, Kentucky, 1789-1830*, 1: np.

[22] Robert R. Shriver, "Livingstons of the Lower Eastern Shore of Maryland as Known to the Middle of the 1800's," Lower Delmarva Genealogical Society and the Research Center for Delmarva History and Culture, *Potpourri from Our Files: Family Records of the Lower Eastern Shore*, Studies in the Lower Eastern Shore, vol. 3 (Salisbury, Maryland: Research Center for Delmarva History and Culture, Salisbury State University, 1997), 113. Shriver writes (p. 116) that the data for James' family comes from notes written on flyleaves of books in the possession of James' son, Joshua Livingston. Shriver does not indicate where researchers may examine the books.

[23] County Clerk, Woodford County, Kentucky, Tax Assessment Book, 1808, James Livingston entry;Kentucky Historical Society, *Tax Books of Kentucky counties,* microfilm 73-0416; Martin F. Schmidt Research Library, Thomas D. Clark Center for Kentucky History, Kentucky Historical Society, Frankfort, Kentucky. James is last listed in 1808, indicating that he may have died. His son, Stephen, first appears in the 1809 tax list for Woodford County.

[24] Shriver, "Livingstons of the Lower Eastern Shore of Maryland," 116.

[25] Shriver, "Livingstons of the Lower Eastern Shore of Maryland," 117.

[26] Shriver, "Livingstons of the Lower Eastern Shore of Maryland," 117.

[27] Joe Slavin, "Descendants of George Livingston, Sr. (First Five Generations), Livingston Family (http://www.hto-livingston.com/ : accessed 5 June 2011). Slavin gives Ellender's birth date as 23 November 1783. However, she gives her age as 54 in the 1850 U.S. census and as 65 in the 1860 U.S. census. Since she supplied the information for the two censuses and since they agree with each other, the census reports more likely contain a more accurate birth year. See 1850 U.S. census, [Part of] Hickman County, Kentucky, p. 92, dwelling 625, family 661, Ellen V. Edrington; digital images, *Ancestry.com* (http://www.Ancestry.com); citing National Archives and Records Administration microfilm M432, roll 205; and 1860 U.S. census, Columbus, Hickman County, Kentucky, p. 465, dwelling 172, family 166, Ellen V. Edrington; digital images, *Ancestry.com* (htttp://www.Ancestry.com); citing National Archives and Records Administration microfilm M653, roll 374.

[28] 1860 U.S. census, Columbus, Hickman County, Kentucky, p. 475, Ellen V. Edrington. Ellen is a widow by 1860.

[29] Shriver, "Livingstons of the Lower Eastern Shore of Maryland," 117, gives 15 October 1791 as her birth date. This may be a misreading of a "6" as a "1." See 1850 U.S. census, [Part of] Hickman County, Kentucky, p. 55 (stamped 28), dwelling 286, family 294, Elizabeth Cook; digital images, *Ancestry.com* (htttp://www.Ancestry.com); citing National Archives and Records Administration microfilm M432, roll 205, where she gives her age as 54; and 1860 U.S. census, Columbus, Hickman County, Kentucky, p. 29, dwelling 264, family 198, Elizabeth Cook; digital images, *Ancestry.com* (htttp://www.Ancestry.com); citing National Archives and Records Administration microfilm M653, roll 374, where she gives her age as 64. Since she likely supplied in the information recorded by the two census takers, and because the two dates are in agreement, 1796 is likely a more accurate date of birth.

[30] 1860 U.S. census, Columbus Hickman County, Kentucky, p. 29, Elizabeth Cook. Elizabeth appears to be a widow by 1860.

[31] Shriver, "Livingstons of the Lower Eastern Shore of Maryland," 116.

[32] Barnes, *The Commonwealth of Missouri*, 770. Martha Livingston indicated that she lived with her grandmother for ten years before she moved to live with her sister Rebecca in neighboring Shelby County. If that time started at age four, by when she had lost both of her parents, then she lived with Sara from 1828-1838. Sara, who would have been 76 years old in 1838, may may have died or have needed care from an older grandchild.

[33] Shriver, "Livingstons of the Lower Eastern Shore of Maryland," 116.

[34] Francis Jackson (Private, Captain Vaughn's Company, Virginia Line, Revolutionary War), Pension Application S.13525 (Act of 1832); Revolutionary War Pension and Bounty-Land Warrant Application Files, Record Group 15; National Archives, Washington, D.C.; digital images, "Revolutionary War Pensions," Footnote.com (http://www.footnote.com/ : accessed 9 June 2011).

[35] Woodford County, Kentucky, Wills Book K: 170, Francis Jackson Inventory, 20 March 1835; Legal Records Department, County Clerk's Office, Versailles, Kentucky. Since the inventory was taken near the end of the month, his death may have occurred near the early part of that month.

[36] Helen S. Hardin of Roanoke, VA, to "Miss Coleman," letter, 13 March 1959; Jackson folder, Surname Files, Martin F. Schmidt Research Library, Thomas D. Clark Center for Kentucky History, Kentucky Historical Society, Frankfort, Kentucky. The letter describes the writer's research findings, including a number of Amelia County marriages.

[37] Helen S. Hardin of Roanoke, VA to "Miss Coleman," letter, 13 March 1959;Jackson folder, Surname Files, Martin F. Schmidt Research Library, Thomas D. Clark Center for Kentucky History, Kentucky Historical Society, Frankfort, Kentucky. The letter describes the writer's research findings, including a number of Amelia County marriages.

[38] Births of the Children of Francis Jackson, Jackson Family Bible.

[39] 1850 U.S. Census, District No. 1, Jefferson County, Kentucky, p. 222B (stamped), dwelling 694, family 695, M. Jackson; digital images, *Ancestry.com* (http://www.Ancestry.com); citing National Archives and Records Administration microfilm M432, roll 205.

[40] Births of the Children of Francis Jackson. Jackson Family Bible. Note that in one instance the given name is spelled "Josiah." In all others it is spelled "Joshua."

[41] Births of the Children of Francis Jackson. Jackson Family Bible.

[42] Births of the Children of Francis Jackson. Jackson Family Bible.

[43] Births of the Children of Francis Jackson. Jackson Family Bible.

[44] Births of the Children of Francis Jackson. Jackson Family Bible.

[45] Births of the Children of Francis Jackson. Jackson Family Bible.

[46] Births of the Children of Francis Jackson. Jackson Family Bible. The source clearly has "Eliza Jackson 2nd June 1795;" however, her sibling Martha is also give as born in 1795. More research is needed to resolve the conflict. I have changed the year to 1796 to make it fit.

[47] Births of the Children of Francis Jackson, Jackson Family Bible.

[48] Births of the Children of Francis Jackson. Jackson Family Bible.

[49] The Will of John Maddera, Jane Ellen Johnson, transcriber, Surry County, Virginia, Wills Book 11: 294; Surry County Wills and Administrations, microfilm 7, The Library of Virginia, Richmond, Virginia; *the Madaris, Medearis, Medaris, McDaris, McDearis, Medaries Family Tree* (http://www.mindspring.com/ ; accessed 9 June 2011).

[50] Helen S. Hardin to "Miss Coleman," letter, 13 March 1959.

Livingston Family Members

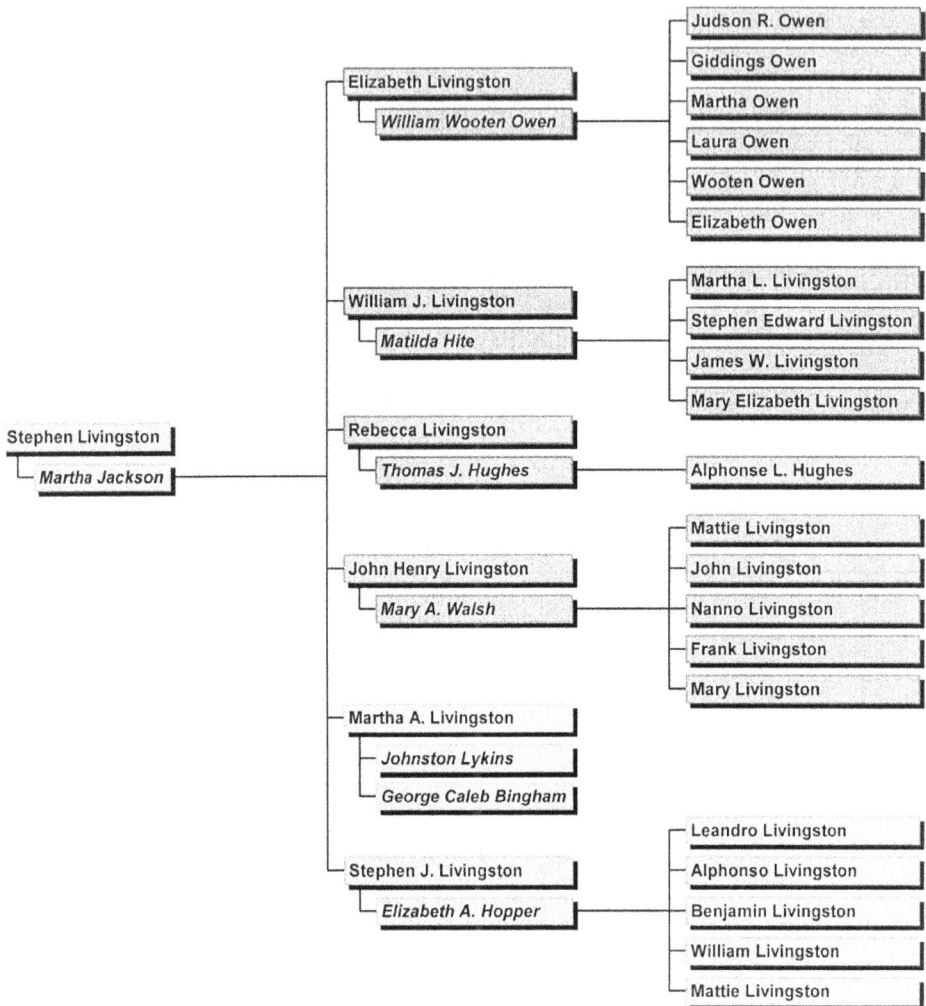

Stephen Livingston — *Martha Jackson*

- **Elizabeth Livingston** — *William Wooten Owen*
  - Judson R. Owen
  - Giddings Owen
  - Martha Owen
  - Laura Owen
  - Wooten Owen
  - Elizabeth Owen
- **William J. Livingston** — *Matilda Hite*
  - Martha L. Livingston
  - Stephen Edward Livingston
  - James W. Livingston
  - Mary Elizabeth Livingston
- **Rebecca Livingston** — *Thomas J. Hughes*
  - Alphonse L. Hughes
- **John Henry Livingston** — *Mary A. Walsh*
  - Mattie Livingston
  - John Livingston
  - Nanno Livingston
  - Frank Livingston
  - Mary Livingston
- **Martha A. Livingston** — *Johnston Lykins* — *George Caleb Bingham*
- **Stephen J. Livingston** — *Elizabeth A. Hopper*
  - Leandro Livingston
  - Alphonso Livingston
  - Benjamin Livingston
  - William Livingston
  - Mattie Livingston

Descendants of
Stephen Livingston and Martha Jackson

First Generation

1. Stephen Livingston, son of **James Livingston** and **Sarah Cathell**, died about 1828 in Kentucky.[1]

Stephen married **Martha Jackson**, daughter of **Francis Jackson** and **Martha Maddera**, on 12 Nov 1812 in Woodford County, Kentucky.[2] Martha died about 1826 in Kentucky.[3]

Children from this marriage were:

+ 2   i.   **Elizabeth Livingston** was born about 1815 in Kentucky[4] and died about 1883 in Shelbyville, Kentucky.[5]

+ 3   ii.   **William J. Livingston** was born about 1819 in Kentucky[6] and died on 19 August 1864 in St. Louis, Missouri.[7]

+ 4   iii.   **John Henry Livingston** was born about 1821 in Kentucky.[8]

+ 5   iv.   **Rebecca Livingston** was born about 1822 in Kentucky.[9]

6   v.   **Martha Ann "Mattie" Livingston** was born in January 1824 in Shelbyville, Shelby County, Kentucky,[10] died on 20 Sep 1890 in Kansas City, Jackson County, Missouri,[11] and was buried on 21 Sep 1890 in Union Cemetery, Kansas City, Jackson County, Missouri.[12]

Martha married **Johnston Lykins**, son of **David L. Lykins** and **Jemima Willis**, on 12 Oct 1851 in Lexington, Lafayette County, Missouri.[13] Johnston was born on 15 Apr 1800 in Franklin County, Virginia,[14] died on

15 August 1876 in Kansas City, Jackson County,
Missouri,[15] and was buried in Union Cemetery, Kansas
City, Jackson County, Missouri.[16]

Martha next married **George Caleb Bingham**, son of
Henry Vest Bingham and **Maria Christiana Amend**, on
18 June 1878 in Kansas City, Jackson County, Missouri.[17]
George was born on 20 Mar 1811 in Augusta County,
Virginia,[18] died on 7 July 1879 in Kansas City, Jackson
County, Missouri,[19] and was buried in July 1879 in Union
Cemetery, Kansas City, Jackson County, Missouri.[20]

+ 7 vi. **Stephen J. Livingston** was born in 1825 in Frankfort,
Franklin County, Kentucky[21] and died before 1880 in
Monmouth Township, Shawnee County, Kansas.[22]

Second Generation (Children)

2. **Elizabeth Livingston** was born in 1815 in Kentucky[23] and died about 1883 in
Shelbyville, Kentucky.[24]

Elizabeth married **William Wooten Owen**, son of **Robert Owen** and **Katherine
Talbot**, on 25 Jan. 1836 in Franklin County, Kentucky.[25] William was born
about 1815 in Kentucky[26] and died before 1870.[27]

Children from this marriage were:

+ 8 i. **Judson R. Owen** was born about 1838 in Kentucky[28]
and died about 1870.[29]

9 ii. **Giddings Owen** was born about 1840 in Kentucky.[30]

10 iii. **Martha Rebecca Owen** was born about 1844 in Kentucky[31]
and died 30 Mar 1881[32]

Martha married **Orlando Raymond Meriwether**, son of **David Meriwether** and
Sarah Leonard, on 2 Nov 1876.[33] Orlando was born on 1 Dec 1830 in
Kentucky, died on 19 Mar 1899 in Asheville, Buncombe, North Carolina, and
was buried in Cave Hill Cemetery, Louisville, Jefferson County, Kentucky.[34]

+   11   iv.   **Laura Owen** was born about 1846 in Kentucky[35] and died after 1900.[36]

     12   v.   **Wooten Owen** was born about 1848 in Kentucky.[37]

+   13   vi.   **Elizabeth Owen** was born 10 Mar 1857 in Jefferson County, Kentucky[38] and died in 1914 in New York.[39]

3. William Jackson Livingston was born in 1819 in Kentucky[40] and died on 19 August 1864 in St. Louis, St. Louis County, Missouri.[41]

William married **Matilda Hite**, daughter of **Joseph Hite** and **Elizabeth Ann Smith Waid**, on 11 Apr 1844 in Shelby County, Kentucky.[42] Matilda was born about 1823 in Kentucky[43] and died 19 June 1891 in Williamsport Township, Shawnee County, Kansas.[44]

Children from this marriage were:

     14   i.   **Martha L. Livingston** was born about 1844 in Kentucky[45] and died between 1880 and 1900.[46]

Martha married **Samuel Golladay** around 1868.[47] Samuel was born in Kentucky in July1839[48] and died in 1906.[49]

     15   ii.   **James W. Livingston** was born in about 1850 in Kentucky,[50] died on 1 Oct 1925 in Wakarusa, Shawnee County, Kansas,[51] and was buried in Yocum Cemetery, Shawnee County, Kansas.[52]

James married **Mary Ellen Yocum** around 1877.[53] Mary was born about 1861 in Shawnee County, Kansas,[54] died in 1932 in Shawnee County, Kansas,[55] and was buried in Yocum Cemetery, Shawnee County, Kansas.[56]

     16   iii.   **Stephen Edward Livingston** was born about 1854 in Kentucky,[57] died in 1935 in Carbondale, Osage County, Kansas,[58] and was buried on 17 Feb 1935 in Yocum Cemetery, Shawnee County, Kansas.[59]

Stephen married **Cora McLaughlin**.[60] Cora was born on 10 Sept 1869 in Shelby County, Indiana,[61] died on 30 Jan. 1946 in Carbondale, Osage County, Kansas,[62] and was buried in Yocum Cemetery, Shawnee County, Kansas.[63]

17	iv.	**Mary Elizabeth Livingston** was born in 1860 in Missouri[64] and died on 6 Dec 1927 in Carbondale, Osage County, Kansas.[65]

Mary married **David French Hercules** by March 1885.[66] David was born in 1849 in Ohio,[67] died in 1905 in Shawnee County, Kansas.[68]

4. John Henry Livingston was born about 1821 in Kentucky.[69]

John married **Mary A. Walsh**, about 1866.[70] Mary was born in July 1842 in Canada.[71]

Children from this marriage were:

18	i.	**Mattie Livingston** was born about 1867 in California.[72]
19	ii.	**John Livingston** was born about 1868 in California.[73]
20	iii.	**Nanno Livingston** was born on 19 Oct 1870 in California.[74]
21	iv.	**Frank Livingston** was born about 1872 in California.[75]
22	v.	**Mary Livingston** was born about 1873 in California.[76]

5. Rebecca Livingston was born about 1822 in Kentucky.[77]

Rebecca married **Thomas J. Hughes**, on 15 Oct 1840 in Lewis County, Missouri.[78] Thomas was born about 1815 in Kentucky[79] and died about 15 Sept 1848 in Waverly, Lafayette County, Missouri.[80]

The children from this marriage was:

23	i.	**Unknown male Hughes** was born between 1840-1848 in Missouri and died after 1890, possibly in Denver, Colorado[81]
24	ii.	**Alphonse L. Hughes** was born about 1846 in Missouri[82] and died on 9 Feb 1894 in Kansas City, Jackson County, Missouri.[83]

7. Stephen J. Livingston was born about 1825 in Frankfort, Franklin County, Kentucky[84] and died before 1880 in Monmouth Township, Shawnee County, Kansas.[85]

Stephen married **Elizabeth A. Hopper**, on 24 June 1852 in Fayette County, Kentucky.[86] Elizabeth was born about 1826 in Fayette County, Kentucky.[87]

Children from this marriage were:

25	i.	**Leander Livingston** was born about 1856 in Kansas.[88]
26	ii.	**Alphonso Livingston** was born about 1860 in Kansas.[89]
27	iii.	**Benjamin Livingston** was born about 1863 in Kansas.[90]
28	iv.	**William Livingston** was born about 1866 in Kansas.[91]
29	v.	**Mattie Livingston** was born about 1870 in Kansas.[92]

Third Generation (Grandchildren)

8. Judson R. Owen was born about 1838 in Kentucky[93] and died in 1870.[94]

Judson married **Albin Smith**.[95] Albin was born on 14 Oct 1844 in Tennessee,[96] died on 31 Jan. 1908 in Nevada County, Arkansas,[97] and was buried in Falcon Cemetery, Buckner, Nevada County, Arkansas.[98]

Children from this marriage were:

30	i.	**Dewit Livingston Owen** was born on 9 Sep 1866 in Louisville, Jefferson County, Kentucky,[99] died 8 Nov 1939 in Kansas City, Jackson County, Missouri,[100] and was buried in Forest Hill Cemetery, Kansas City, Jackson County, Missouri.[101]

Dewit married **Ada Armintha Campbell**, daughter of **Stephen Campbell** and **Amanda --?--**, on 26 June 1902 in Kansas City, Jackson County, Missouri.[102] Ada was born in 13 Dec 1881 in Loveland, Pottawattamie County, Iowa[103] and died in 4 July 1971 in Kansas City, Jackson County, Missouri.[104]

31	ii.	**William Owen** was born about 1868 in Tennessee[105] and died about 1915 in Texas.[106]

William married **Mabel --?--**. Mabel was born in March 1876 in Texas[107] and died on 25 Jan. 1973 in Harris County, Texas.[108]

    32   iii.   **L. L. Owen** was born in 1870.[109]

11. Laura Owen was born about 1846 in Kentucky[110] and died after 1900.[111]

Laura married **Isaac C. Mills** about 1870.[112] Isaac was born in January 1840 in New York[113] and died after 1900.[114]

The child from this marriage was:

    34   i.   **May L. Mills** was born in December 1876 in New York.[115]

13. Elizabeth Owen was born about 10 Mar 1857 in Jefferson County, Kentucky[116] and died in 1914 in New York.[117]

Elizabeth married **John Alan Campbell**.[118] John was born about 1835 in Maryland[119] and died in 1899 in New York.[120]

The child from this marriage was:

    35   i.   **Charlotte Campbell** was born about 1878 in Cumberland, Allegany County, Maryland.[121]

Charlotte married **Everett Ryder** about 1905.[122] Everett was born about 1876 in New York.[123]

Fourth Generation (Great-Grandchildren)

30. Dewit Livingston Owen was born on 9 Sept 1866 in Louisville, Kentucky,[124] died 8 Nov 1939 in Kansas City, Jackson County, Missouri,[125] and was buried in Union Cemetery, Kansas City, Jackson County, Missouri.[126]

Dewit married **Ada Armintha Campbell**, daughter of **Stephen Campbell** and **Amanda --?--**, on 26 June 1902 in Kansas City, Missouri.[127] Ada was born in 13 Dec 1880 in Loveland, Pottawattamie County, Iowa[128] and died in 4 July 1971 in Kansas City, Jackson County, Missouri.[129]

The child from this marriage was:

+ 36   i.   **Kenneth Campbell Owen** was born on 23 Nov 1914 in Kansas City, Jackson County, Missouri[130] and died on 18 Jun 1969 in Leawood, Johnson County, Kansas.[131]

31. William Owen was born about 1868 in Tennessee[132] and died about 1915 in Texas.[133]

William married **Mabel --?--**. Mabel was born about 1896 in Texas[134] and died on 25 Jan 1973 in Harris, Texas.[135]

Children from this marriage were:

37   i.   **Polly Owen** was born about 1914 in Texas.[136].

38   ii.   **Ilona Owen** was born about 1915 in Texas.[137]

35. Charlotte Campbell was born about 1878 in Cumberland, Maryland.[138]

Charlotte married **Everett Ryder**. Everett was born about 1876 in New York.[139]

The child from this marriage was:

39   i.   **Everett Owen Ryder** was born on 26 Jul 1906 in New York[140] and died on 25 Sep 1988 in Ventura, California.[141]

Fifth Generation (Great Great-Grandchildren)

36. Kenneth Campbell Owen was born on 23 Nov 1914 in Kansas City, Jackson County, Missouri[142] and died on 18 Jun 1969 in Leawood, Johnson County, Kansas.[143]

Kenneth married **Mary Elenor Fish** on 18 Jun 1942.[144] Mary was born on 26 Apr 1921 in St. Louis, Missouri.[145]

The child from this marriage was:

40   i.   **Robert Dewit Owen**[146] was born on 15 Nov 1948 in St. Louis, Missouri.[147]

[1] Ermina Jett Darnell, *Forks of Elkhorn Church with Genealogies of Early Members* (Louisville, Kentucky: Standard Printing, 1946), 179, 190. . See also Dodd Jordan, "Kentucky Marriages, 1802-1850," database, *Ancestry.com* (http://www.ancestry.com/search : accessed 29 November 2010), entry for Stephen Livingston and Martha Jackson.

[2] Ermina Jett Darnell, *Forks of Elkhorn Church with Genealogies of Early Members* (Louisville, Kentucky: Standard Printing, 1946), 179, 190. . See also Dodd Jordan, "Kentucky Marriages, 1802-1850," database, *Ancestry.com* (http://www.ancestry.com/search : accessed 29 November 2010), entry for Stephen Livingston and Martha Jackson.

[3] *The History of Jackson County, Missouri*, 741.

[4] 1870 U.S. census, Louisville, Jefferson County, Kentucky, p. 288, dwelling 1838, family 2315, Elizabeth Owen; digital image, *Ancestry.com* (http://www.ancestry.com : accessed 5 September 2010).

[5] "Mrs. M.A. Bingham is Dead. Quietly Peacefully a Remarkable Woman Passes Away." *Kansas City* (Mo.) *Times,* 21 Sept. 1890, p. 6, c. 1.

[6] 1850 U.S. census, District no. 2, Shelby County, Kentucky, p. 374 (stamped), dwelling 480, family 494; digital image, *Ancestry.com* (http://www.ancestry.com/ : accessed 8 September 2010); citing National Archives and Records Administration microfilm M432, roll 218. See also Darnell, *Forks of Elkhorn Church*, 190.

[7] Missouri State Archives, "Missouri's Union Provost Marshal Records, 1861-1866," database, *Missouri Digital Heritage* (http://www.sos.mo.gov/archives/provost/ : accessed 25 August 2010), report of H. H. Williams to Col. Sanderson reporting hanging of William Jackson Livingston.

[8] 1860 U.S. census, Township No. 1, Contra Costa County, California, p. 55, dwelling 435, family 435, John H. Livingston; digital image, *Ancestry.com* (http://www.ancestry.com/ : accessed 8 September 2010); citing National Archives and Records Administration microfilm M653, roll 57. John H. Livingston was the census enumerator for this township.

[9] Franklin County, Kentucky, Circuit Court, Settlement Book B: 287; Rebecca Livingston, 3 August 1842; County Clerk's Office, Frankfort, Kentucky. In this document, her guardian settles his account with Rebecca, giving her the inheritance she was due from the estates of Francis Jackson and Stephen Livingston. Assuming that her guardian gave her the inheritance within a month of her turning 21, we can infer that she was born around July, 1821. (See *Century Edition of the American Digest: a Complete Digest of All Reported American Cases from the Earliest Times to 1896* (St. Paul, Minnesota: West Publishing, 1901), 27:971, para. 3[b], citing Harris v. Berry, 6 Ky.L.Rep.157.)

[10] C. R. Barnes, ed., *The Commonwealth of Missouri: A Centennial Record* (Saint Louis: Bryan, Brand & Company, 1877), 770. Mattie Livingston was still alive when Barnes assembled material for his book. He may have interviewed her for his section on Mattie.

[11] Missouri State Archives, "Missouri birth and Death Records Database, Pre-1910," database, *Missouri Digital Heritage* (http://www.sos.mo.gov.archives/resources/birthdeath/ : accessed 27 Nov 2010), Death of Bingham, Martha A.

[12] Union Cemetery Historical Society, *Tombstone Inscriptions* (Kansas City: Union Cemetery Historical Society, 1986), 8.

[13] C. R. Barnes, *The Commonwealth of Missouri*, 770.

[14] For date, see Lykins Family Bible (SC33-2), Missouri Valley Special Collections, Kansas City Public Library, Kansas City, Missouri. The Bible was that of Dr. Lykins' parents. For place, see "Johnston Lykins and Delilah McCoy Family Group Sheet," Johnston Lykins and Martha Lykins Bingham Papers, KC-0294; Native Sons of Greater Kansas City Archives, State Historical Society of Missouri Research Center-Kansas City, Kansas City, Missouri.

[15] Fred Lee, "Genealogical Background of Dr. Johnston Lykins," *Kansas City Genealogist* 36 (Winter, Spring, 1985): 125.

[16] Union Cemetery Historical Society, *Tombstone Inscriptions* (Kansas City: Union Cemetery Historical Society, 1986), 53.

[17] Paul C. Nagel, *George Caleb Bingham: Missouri's Famed Painter and Forgotten Politician* (Columbia, Missouri: University of Missouri Press, 2005), 146.

[18] .Nagel, *George Caleb Bingham*, 1-2.

[19] Nagel, *George Caleb Bingham*, 150.

[20] Union Cemetery Historical Society, *Tombstone Inscriptions* (Kansas City: Union Cemetery Historical Society, 1986), 8.

[21] 1850 U.S. census, District no. 1, Franklin County, Kentucky, p. 20 (stamped), dwelling and family 261, Stephen J. Livingston; digital image, *Ancestry.com* (http://www.ancestry.com/ : accessed 8 September 2010); citing National Archives and Records Administration microfilm M432, roll 200.

[22] 1880 U.S. census, Monmouth, Shawnee County, Kansas, ED 16, p. 5, dwelling and family 34, Lizzie Livingston [widow]; digital image, *Ancestry.com* (http://www.ancestry.com/ : accessed 8 September 2010); citing National Archives and Records Administration microfilm T9, roll 397.

[23] 1870 U.S. census, Louisville, Jefferson County, Kentucky, p. 288, dwelling 1838, family 2315, Elizabeth Owen; digital image, *Ancestry.com* (http://www.ancestry.com : accessed 5 September 2010).

[24] "Mrs. M.A. Bingham is Dead," 6.

[25] CD229 Jean Ladd and Rhea Meigs, comps., "Marriage Records in Southern States," CD 229; CD-ROM database, (Logan, Utah: Everton Publishers, nd). See also Daughters of the American Revolution, "Descendants Database," *DAR Genealogical Research System* (http://services.dar.org/Public/DAR_Research/ : accessed 10 December 2010), Charlotte A. Ryder application, no. 164792, descendant of Brackett Owen. The applicant was the granddaughter of Elizabeth Livingston.

[26] 1850 U.S. census, District no. 2, Shelby County, Kentucky, p. 384 (stamped) (verso), dwelling 658, family 675, W. W. Owen; digital image, *Ancestry.com* (http://ancestry.com/ : accessed 28 November 2010); citing National Archives and Records Administration microfilm M432, roll 218.

[27] 1870 U.S. census, Louisville, Jefferson County, Kentucky, p. 288, dwelling 1838, family 2315, Elizabeth Owen; digital image, *Ancestry.com* (http://ancestry.com/ : accessed 28 November 2010); citing National Archives and Records Administration microfilm M593, roll 476.

[28] 1850 U.S. census, District no. 2, Shelby County, Kentucky, p. 384 (stamped) (verso), dwelling 658, family 675, Judson Owen; digital image, *Ancestry.com* (http://ancestry.com/ : accessed 28 November 2010); citing National Archives and Records Administration microfilm M432, roll 218.

[29] His wife Albin's application for a widow's pension was filed in Washington on 6 October 1869, yet he is listed in the 1870 census taken on 7 July 1870. In spite of the conflict in dates, it is reasonable to conclude that he died around 1870. "Civil War and Later Veterans Pension Index," Judson R. Owens [sic], Cont. Sgn., Med. Dept. U.S. Vols., widow's application no. 199793, 6 October 1869, *Footnote.com* (http://www.footnote.com/ : accessed 15 September 2010); citing National Archives and Records Administration microfilm T289, roll 747. 1870 U.S. census, Pine Tavern District, Bullitt County, Kentucky, p. 27, dwelling and family 192; digital image, *Ancestry.com* (http://www.ancestry.com : accessed 15 November 2010).

[30] 1850 U.S. census, District no. 2, Shelby County, Kentucky, p. 384 (stamped) (verso), dwelling 658, family 675, Giddings Owen; digital image, *Ancestry.com* (http://ancestry.com/ : accessed 28 November 2010); citing National Archives and Records Administration microfilm M432, roll 218.

[31] 1850 U.S. census, District no. 2, Shelby County, Kentucky, p. 384 (stamped) (verso), dwelling 658, family 675, Martha Owen; digital image, *Ancestry.com* (http://ancestry.com/ : accessed 28 November 2010); citing National Archives and Records Administration microfilm M432, roll 218.

[32] Leonard, Manning. *Memorial, genealogical, historical and biographical of Solomon Leonard, 1637, of Duxbury and Bridgewater, Massachussetts, and some of his descendants* (unknown: unknown, 1896), 337.

[33] Leonard, 337.

[34] North Carolina Family Search, State Death Registers, (Not Given), FHL microfilm item 412574.

[35] 1850 U.S. census, District no. 2, Shelby County, Kentucky, p. 384 (verso); dwelling 658, family 675, Laura Owen; digital image, *Ancestry.com* (http://ancestry.com/ : accessed 28 November 2010) citing National Archives and Records Administration microfilm M432, roll 218.

[36] 1900 U.S. census, Brooklyn, Kings County, New York, ED 405, sheet 2A, dwelling 25, family 27; digital image, *Ancestry.com* (http://www.ancestry.com/ ; accessed 29 November 2010); citing National Archives and Records Administration microfilm T623, roll T6061.

[37] 1850 U.S. census, District no. 2, Shelby County, Kentucky, p. 384 (stamped) (verso), dwelling 658, family 675, Wooton Owen; digital image, *Ancestry.com* (http://ancestry.com/ : accessed 28 November 2010); citing National Archives and Records Administration microfilm M432, roll 218.

[38] Ancestry.com, "Kentucky Birth Records, 1852-1910," np, Elizabeth Owen, digital image, *Ancestry.com* (http://ancestry.com/ : accessed 28 November 2010); citing Kentucky Department of Libraries and Archives microfilm set 994027-994058. See also Daughters of the American Revolution, "Descendants Database," *DAR Genealogical Research System* (http://services.dar.org/Public/DAR_Research/ : accessed 10 December 2010), Charlotte A. Ryder application, no. 164792, descendant of Brackett Owen. The applicant was the granddaughter of Elizabeth Livingston.

[39] Daughters of the American Revolution, "Descendants Database," *DAR Genealogical Research System* (http://services.dar.org/Public/DAR_Research/ : accessed 10 December 2010), Charlotte A. Ryder application, no. 164792, descendant of Brackett Owen. The applicant was the granddaughter of Elizabeth Livingston.

[40] 1850 U.S. census, District no. 2, Shelby County, Kentucky, p. 374 (stamped), dwelling 480, family 494; digital image, *Ancestry.com* (http://www.ancestry.com/ : accessed 8 September 2010); citing National Archives and Records Administration microfilm M432, roll 218. See also Darnell, *Forks of Elkhorn Church*, 190.

[41] Missouri State Archives, "Missouri's Union Provost Marshal Records, 1861-1866," database, *Missouri Digital Heritage* (http://www.sos.mo.gov/archives/provost/ : accessed 25 August 2010), report of H. H. Williams to Col. Sanderson reporting hanging of William Jackson Livingston.

[42] Eula Richardson Hasskarl, *Shelby County, Kentucky Marriages* (Ada, Oklahoma: Eula Richardson Hasskarl, 1985), 2: 52. The entries in the book are abstracts made from microfilmed copies of the original records held at the Kentucky Historical Society. The record does not name the parents of the groom and only the father of the bride. Names of the bridal

couple's parents come from a descendant. See Larry Lynn Livingston Kansas 1950, Public Member Trees; Ancestry.com (http://www.ancestry.com/ : accessed 12 December 2010), William Jackson Livingston—Matilda Hite family group sheet.

[43] 1850 U.S. census, District no. 2, Shelby County, Kentucky, p. 374 (stamped), dwelling 480, family 494, Matilda Livingston; digital image, *Ancestry.com* (http://www.ancestry.com ; accessed 27 November 2010); citing National Archives and Records Administration microfilm M432, roll 218.

[44] Cora McLaughlin Livingston Family Bible, privately held by Larry Livingston, Carbondale, Kansas.

[45] 1850 U.S. census, District no. 2, Shelby County, Kentucky, p. 374 (stamped), dwelling 480, family 494; digital image, *Ancestry.com* (http://www.ancestry.com/ : accessed 8 September 2010); citing National Archives and Records Administration microfilm M432, roll 218.

[46] 1880 U.S. census, Roaring Spring, Trigg County, Kentucky, ED 149, p. 4, line 17, Hattie Golladay; digital image, *Ancestry.com* (http://www.ancestry.com/ : accessed 8 September 2010); citing National Archives and Records Administration microfilm T9, roll 443. 1900 U.S. census, Roaring Spring, Trigg County, Kentucky, ED 85, sheet 18A, dwelling and family 347, Sam Golidy; digital image, *Ancestry.com* (http://www.ancestry.com/ : accessed 8 September 2010); citing National Archives and Records Administration microfilm T623, roll 552.

[47] 1870 U.S. census, Roaring Spring, Trigg County, Kentucky, p. 43, dwelling and family 322, Martha L. Godiday; digital image, *Ancestry.com* (http://www.ancestry.com/ : accessed 8 September 2010); citing National Archives and Records Administration microfilm M593, roll 501. The couple's oldest child, William, was one year old, suggesting a marriage around 1869. Descendant Larry Lynn Livingston does not supply a source for Martha's marriage to Samuel. Thus, Samuel's wife may not be this Martha Livingston. See Larry Lynn Livingston Kansas 1950, Public Member Trees; Ancestry.com (http://www.ancestry.com/ : accessed 12 December 2010), Samuel Golladay—Martha Livingston family group sheet.

[48] 1900 U.S. census, Roaring Spring, Trigg County, Kentucky, ED 85, sheet 18A, dwelling and family 347, Sam Golidy; digital image, *Ancestry.com* (http://www.ancestry.com/ : accessed 8 September 2010); citing National Archives and Records Administration microfilm T623, roll 552.

[49] Larry Lynn Livingston Kansas 1950, Public Member Trees; Ancestry.com (http://www.ancestry.com/ : accessed 12 December 2010), Samuel Golladay—Martha Livingston family group sheet.

[50] 1860 U.S. census, South River Township, Marion County, Missouri, p. 58, dwelling 367, family 388, James W. Livingston; digital image, *Ancestry.com* (http://www.ancestry.com/ : accessed 8 September 2010); citing National Archives and Records Administration microfilm M653, roll 632.

[51] "Aged Man is Dead. James Livingston Stricken While Inspecting Corn Field," clipping dated 10-1-1925 from unidentified newspaper; Livingston family papers in possession of Larry Lynn Livingston, Carbondale, Kansas.

[52] Aged Man is Dead. James Livingston Stricken While Inspecting Corn Field," clipping dated 10-1-1925 from unidentified newspaper; Livingston family papers in possession of Larry Lynn Livingston, Carbondale, Kansas.

[53] 1880 U.S. census, Williamsport Township, Shawnee County, Kansas, ED 11, p. 11, dwelling 105, family 112, J. and Mary Livingston; ☺ digital image, *Ancestry.com* (http://www.ancestry.com/ : accessed 8 September 2010); citing National Archives and Records Administration microfilm T9, roll 397. Their oldest child was two years old when the census taker came by, suggesting a marriage around 1877.

[54] 1875 Kansas State census, Williamsport Township, Shawnee County, Kansas, p. 1, dwelling and family 5, Mary E. Yocum; digital image, Ancestry.com (http://www.ancestry.com/ : accessed 1 December 2010); citing Kansas State Historical Society microfilm K-1 through K-20.

[55] Joan Hrenchir, "Yocum Cemetery," Shawnee County, Kansas, entry for Mary Ellen Yocum Livingston; database, "The Tombstone Transcription Project," USGenWeb (http://www.usgwtombstones.org/kansas/shawnee.htm : accessed 11 December 2010).

[56] Joan Hrenchir, "Yocum Cemetery," Shawnee County, Kansas, entry for Mary Ellen Yocum Livingston; database, "The Tombstone Transcription Project," USGenWeb (http://www.usgwtombstones.org/kansas/shawnee.htm : accessed 11 December 2010).

[57] 1860 U.S. census, South River Township, Marion County, Missouri, p. 58, dwelling 367, family 388, Steven E. Livingston; digital image, Ancestry.com (http://www.ancestry.com/ : accessed 8 September 2010); citing National Archives and Records Administration microfilm M653, roll 632.

[58] Joan Hrenchir, "Yocum Cemetery," Shawnee County, Kansas, Edward Livingston; database, "The Tombstone Transcription Project," USGenWeb (http://www.usgwtombstones.org/kansas/shawnee.htm : accessed 11 December 2010). He likely died in Carbondale, Osage County, Kansas, since he was living there only five years earlier. See 1930 U.S. census, Carbondale, Osage County, Kansas, ED 70-18, sheet 3B, dwelling and family 101, S. Edward Livingston; digital image, Ancestry.com (http://www.ancestry.com/ : accessed 8 September 2010); citing National Archives and Records Administration microfilm T626, roll 714.

[59] Joan Hrenchir, "Yocum Cemetery," Shawnee County, Kansas, entry for Edward Livingston; database, "The Tombstone Transcription Project," USGenWeb (http://www.usgwtombstones.org/kansas/shawnee.htm : accessed 11 December 2010).

[60] 1900 U.S. census, Monmouth, Shawnee County, Kansas, ED 134, sheet 4A, dwelling 59, family 61, Edward and Cora Livingston; digital image, Ancestry.com (http://www.ancestry.com/ : accessed 8 September 2010); citing National Archives and Records Administration microfilm T623, roll 500. The couple had been married for fifteen years when the census taker came by.

[61] Standard Certificate of Death, certificate no. 70-6022, Cora May Livingston; photocopy, Division of Vital Statistics, Kansas State Board of Health, Topeka, Kansas.

[62] Standard Certificate of Death, certificate no. 70-6022, Cora May Livingston; photocopy, Division of Vital Statistics, Kansas State Board of Health, Topeka, Kansas.

[63] Joan Hrenchir, "Yocum Cemetery," Shawnee County, Kansas, entry for Cora Livingston; database, "The Tombstone Transcription Project," USGenWeb (http://www.usgwtombstones.org/kansas/shawnee.htm : accessed 11 December 2010).

[64] 1860 U.S. census, South River Township, Marion County, Missouri, p. 58, dwelling 367, family 388, Mary E. Livingston; digital image, Ancestry.com (http://www.ancestry.com/ : accessed 8 September 2010); citing National Archives and Records Administration microfilm M653, roll 632.

[65] "Mrs. Minnie Hercules," clipping, Topeka State Journal, 7 December 1927, np; Livingston family papers in possession of Larry Lynn Livingston, Carbondale, Kansas.

[66] 1885 Kansas State census, Williamsport, Shawnee County, p. 55, dwelling 111, family 114, David and Mary Hercules; digital image, Ancestry.com (http://www.ancestry.com / : accessed 25 November 2010); citing Kansas State Historical Society microfilm KS1885, roll 130. The census was to be taken on the 1st of March in 1885.

[67] 1850 U.S. census, York Township, Darke County, Ohio, p. 470 (stamped) (verso), dwelling and family 71, David Hercules; digital image, *Ancestry.com* (http://www.ancestry.com/ : accessed 8 September 2010); citing National Archives and Records Administration microfilm M432, roll 674.

[68] Larry Livingston, "Larry Lynn Livingston Kansas 1950"; digital images, Ancestry.com, *"Family Trees"* (accessed 8 Dec 2010).

[69] 1860 U.S. census, Township No. 1, Contra Costa County, California, p. 55, dwelling 435, family 435, John H. Livingston; digital image, *Ancestry.com* (http://www.ancestry.com/ : accessed 8 September 2010); citing National Archives and Records Administration microfilm M653, roll 57.

[70] 1870 U.S. census, Township Two, Contra Costa County, California, p. 1, dwelling and family 8, John and Mary A. Livingston; digital image, *Ancestry.com* (http://www..ancestry.com ; accessed 28 November 2010); citing National Archives and Records Administration microfilm M593, roll 71. Their oldest child is three years old, suggesting a marriage around 1866.

[71] 1900 U.S. census, San Jose, Santa Clara County, California, ED 67, sheet 8B, dwelling 191, family 201, Mary A. Livingston; digital image, *Ancestry.com* (http://www.ancestry.com/ : accessed 8 September 2010); citing National Archives and Records Administration microfilm T623 roll 111. See also 1851 Canadian census, Burleigh and Drummer, Peterborough County, Canada West [Ontario], Schedule A, p. 61, line 11, Mary Walsh; digital image, *Ancestry.com* (http://www.ancestry.com/ : accessed 8 September 2010); citing Library and Archives Canada microfilm C-11748. Note that she claims to be born in Ireland in the 1870 and 1880 U.S. censuses.

[72] 1870 U.S. census, Township Two, Contra Costa County, California, p. 1, dwelling and family 8, Mattie Livingston; digital image, *Ancestry.com* (http://www..ancestry.com ; accessed 28 November 2010); citing National Archives and Records Administration microfilm M593, roll 71.

[73] 1870 U.S. census, Township Two, Contra Costa County, California, p. 1, dwelling and family 8, John J. Livingston; digital image, *Ancestry.com* (http://www..ancestry.com ; accessed 28 November 2010); citing National Archives and Records Administration microfilm M593, roll 71.

[74] 1880 U.S. census, Township One, Contra Costa County, California, ED 45, p. 15, dwelling and family 121, Nanno Livingston [widow]; digital image, *Ancestry.com* (http://www.ancestry.com/ : accessed 8 September 2010); citing National Archives and Records Administration microfilm T9, roll 74.

[75] 1880 U.S. census, Township One, Contra Costa County, California, ED 45, p. 15, dwelling and family 121, Frank Livingston [widow]; digital image, *Ancestry.com* (http://www.ancestry.com/ : accessed 8 September 2010); citing National Archives and Records Administration microfilm T9, roll 74.

[76] 1880 U.S. census, Township One, Contra Costa County, California, ED 45, p. 15, dwelling and family 121, Mary Livingston [widow]; digital image, *Ancestry.com* (http://www.ancestry.com/ : accessed 8 September 2010); citing National Archives and Records Administration microfilm T9, roll 74.

[77] 1850 U.S. census, District no. 1, Nicholas County, Kentucky, p. 478 (stamped), dwelling 440, family 442, Rebecca Hughes; digital image, *Ancestry.com* (http://www.ancestry.com/ : accessed 8 September 2010); citing National Archives and Records Administration microfilm M432, roll 215.

[78] Jordan Dodd, "Missouri Marriages to 1850," database, Ancestry.com (http://www.ancestry.com/search : accessed 29 November 2010), entry for Thomas J. Hughes and Rebecca Livingston.

[79] 1850 U.S. census, District no. 1, Nicholas County, Kentucky, p. 478 (stamped), dwelling 440, family 442, Thomas A. [sic] Hughes; digital image, *Ancestry.com* (http://www.ancestry.com/ : accessed 8 September 2010); citing National Archives and Records Administration microfilm M432, roll 215.

[80] Jacqueline Hogan Williams, *Lafayette County, Missouri Abstract of Wills and Administrations, 1821-1850* (Warrensburg, Missouri: Jacqueline Hogan Williams, 1968), 48.

[81] "Mrs. M.A. Bingham is Dead," 6. Source indicates that this nephew of Martha L. Bingham was an attorney in Denver, Colorado.

[82] 1870 U.S. Census, Kansas City Ward 3, Jackson, Missouri,: Roll: M593-782; Page 599B, Image: 608, Family History Library Film: 552281, dwelling 251, family 258, Johns[t]on Lykins; digital image, *Ancestry.com* (http://www.ancestry.com/: accessed 5 May 2011); citing National Archives and Records Administration microfilm M593. Information in other censuses and in his death record supply varying years for his birth year and consistently report his state of birth as Missouri.

[83] Missouri State Archives, "Missouri Birth and Death Records Database," entry for Alphonso L. Hughes; database, *Missouri Digital Heritage* (http://www.sos.mo.gov/archives/ : accessed 25 August 2010); citing Missouri Bureau of Vital Records microfilm C 19509, no. 180.

[84] 1850 U.S. census, District no. 1, Franklin County, Kentucky, p. 20 (stamped), dwelling and family 261, Stephen J. Livingston; digital image, *Ancestry.com* (http://www.ancestry.com/ : accessed 8 September 2010); citing National Archives and Records Administration microfilm M432, roll 200. For documentation of his county of birth, see "Kentucky Marriage Records, 1852-1914," entry for S. J. Livingston and Elizabeth A. Hopper; digital image, *Ancestry.com* (http://www.ancestry.com/ : accessed 8 September 2010).

[85] 1880 U.S. census, Monmouth, Shawnee County, Kansas, ED 16, p. 5, dwelling and family 34, Lizzie Livingston [widow]; digital image, *Ancestry.com* (http://www.ancestry.com/ : accessed 8 September 2010); citing National Archives and Records Administration microfilm T9, roll 397.

[86] "Kentucky Marriage Records, 1852-1914," entry for S. J. Livingston and Elizabeth A. Hopper; digital image, *Ancestry.com* (http://www.ancestry.com/ : accessed 8 September 2010).

[87] "Kentucky Marriage Records, 1852-1914," entry for S. J. Livingston and Elizabeth A. Hopper; digital image, *Ancestry.com* (http://www.ancestry.com/ : accessed 8 September 2010).

[88] 1860 U.S. census, Monmouth, Shawnee County, Kansas, p. 58, dwelling 536, family 487, Leander Livingston; digital image, *Ancestry.com* (http://www.ancestry.com/ ; accessed 28 November 2010); citing National Archives and Records Administration microfilm M593, roll M653, roll 352.

[89] 1860 U.S. census, Monmouth, Shawnee County, Kansas, p. 58, dwelling 536, family 487, Alphonso Livingston; digital image, *Ancestry.com* (http://www.ancestry.com/ ; accessed 28 November 2010); citing National Archives and Records Administration microfilm M593, roll M653, roll 352.

[90] 1870 U.S. census, Monmouth, Shawnee County, Kansas, p. 16, dwelling 106, family 107, Benjamin Livingston; digital image, *Ancestry.com* (http://www..ancestry.com ; accessed 28 November 2010); citing National Archives and Records Administration microfilm M593, roll 442.

[91] 1870 U.S. census, Monmouth, Shawnee County, Kansas, p. 16, dwelling 106, family 107, William Livingston; digital image, *Ancestry.com* (http://www..ancestry.com ; accessed 28 November 2010); citing National Archives and Records Administration microfilm M593, roll 442.

[92] 1870 U.S. census, Monmouth, Shawnee County, Kansas, p. 16, dwelling 106, family 107, Mattie Livingston; digital image, *Ancestry.com* (http://www..ancestry.com ; accessed 28 November 2010); citing National Archives and Records Administration microfilm M593, roll 442.

[93] 1850 U.S. census, District no. 2, Shelby County, Kentucky, p. 384 (stamped) (verso), dwelling 658, family 675, Judson Owen; digital image, *Ancestry.com* (http://ancestry.com/ : accessed 28 November 2010); citing National Archives and Records Administration microfilm M432, roll 218.

[94] His wife Albin's application for a widow's pension was filed in Washington on 6 October 1869, yet he is listed in the 1870 census taken on 7 July 1870. In spite of the conflict in dates, it is reasonable to conclude that he died around 1870. "Civil War and Later Veterans Pension Index," Judson R. Owens [sic], Cont. Sgn., Med. Dept. U.S. Vols., widow's application no. 199793, 6 October 1869, *Footnote.com* (http://www.footnote.com/ : accessed 15 September 2010); citing National Archives and Records Administration microfilm T289, roll 747. 1870 U.S. census, Pine Tavern District, Bullitt County, Kentucky, p. 27, dwelling and family 192; digital image, *Ancestry.com* (http://www.ancestry.com : accessed 15 November 2010).

[95] Jordan R. Dodd, "Tennessee Marriages, 1851-1900," database, *Ancestry.com* (http://www.ancestry.com/ : accessed 27 November 2010), J. R. Owen – Albin Smith entry.

[96] Jerry and Jeanie McKinley, "Falcon Cemetery—Old Section," Nevada County Cemeteries, *Arkansas Gene* (http://www.argenweb.net/ : accessed 10 December 2010), entry for Albin Ratliffe. See also 1870 U.S. census, Pine Tavern District, Bullitt County, Kentucky, p. 27, dwelling 191, family 191, Albian [sic] Owen; digital image, *Ancestry.com* (http://www.ancestry.com/ : accessed 27 November 2010); citing National Archives and Records Administration microfilm M593, roll 450.

[97] Jerry and Jeanie McKelvy, "Falcon Cemetery—Old Section," Nevada County Cemeteries, *Arkansas GenWeb* (http://www.argenweb.net/ : accessed 10 December 2010), entry for Albin Ratliffe. After Judson's death in 1870, Albin married John M. Radliff. See Brenda Shaw Woods, comp., "Marriage Records," Bullitt County, *Kentucky GenWeb* Archives (http://www.usgwarchives.net/ky/bullitt/ : accessed 10 December 2010), Alvina Owen – John M. Ratcliffe marriage, 14 August 1872.

[98] Jerry and Jeanie McKelvy, "Falcon Cemetery—Old Section," Nevada County Cemeteries, *Arkansas GenWeb* (http://www.argenweb.net/ : accessed 10 December 2010), entry for Albin Ratliffe.

[99] 1870 U.S. census, Pine Tavern District, Bullitt County, Kentucky, p. 29, dwelling 199 and family 199, Dewit Owen; digital image, *Ancestry.com* (http://ancestry.com ; accessed 28 November 2010); citing National Archives and Records Administration microfilm M593, roll 593. See also Bureau of Vital Statistics, Missouri State Board of Health, Certificate of Death, file no. 38528, DeWitt Owen, 8 November 1939; digital image, Missouri State Archives, "Missouri Death Certificates, 1910-1960," Missouri Digital Heritage, Missouri Office of the Secretary of State (http://www.sos.mo.gov/mdh/ : accessed 8 December 2007).

[100] Bureau of Vital Statistics, Missouri State Board of Health, Certificate of Death, file no. 38528, DeWitt Owen, 8 November 1939; digital image, Missouri State Archives, "Missouri

Death Certificates, 1910-1960," Missouri Digital Heritage, Missouri Office of the Secretary of State (http://www.sos.mo.gov/mdh/ : accessed 8 December 2007).

[101] Bureau of Vital Statistics, Missouri State Board of Health, Certificate of Death, file no. 38528, DeWitt Owen, 8 November 1939; digital image, Missouri State Archives, "Missouri Death Certificates, 1910-1960," Missouri Digital Heritage, Missouri Office of the Secretary of State (http://www.sos.mo.gov/mdh/ : accessed 8 December 2007).

[102] Ada Campbell Owen, "Thumbnail Biography," *The Kansas City Genealogist* 25 (Winter, Spring 1985): 121.

Recorder of Deeds, Jackson County, M issouri, Marriage License no. 24627, DeWitt Owen and Ada Campbell, 26 June 1902; digital image, Jackson County Recorder of Deeds (http://jacksongov.org : accessed 29 November 2010).

[103] 1885 Iowa State Census, Grant, Woodbury County, Iowa, p. 102, dwelling and family 94, Ada Campbell; online database, *Ancestry.com* (htpp://ancestry.com : accessed 8 Dec 2010). See also 1900 U.S. census, Esculapia Township, Benton County, Arkansas, ED 11, sheet 18-B, dwelling 379, family 395, Stephen Campbell family; digital image, *Ancestry.com* (http://ancestry.com ; accessed 28 November 2010); citing National Archives and Records Administration microfilm T623, roll 50. See also Robert Dewit Owen, New York to David W. Jackson, e-mail, 9 Feb 2011, "Mattie Lykins Bingham Genealogy"; privately held by Jackson.

[104] Social Security Administration, "Social Security Death Index," database, *Rootsweb.Ancestry.com* (http://www.rootsweb.ancestry.com : accessed 10 December 2010), entry for Ada Owen, SS no. 486-03-1355. See also Robert Dewit Owen, New York to David W. Jackson, e-mail, 9 Feb 2011, "Mattie Lykins Bingham Genealogy"; privately held by Jackson.

[105] 1870 U.S. census, Pine Tavern District, Bullitt County, Kentucky, p. 28, dwelling and family 191, William Owen; digital image, *Ancestry.com* (http://www..ancestry.com/ : accessed 19 November 2010); citing National Archives and Records Administration microfilm M593, roll 450.

[106] 1930 U.S. census, Precinct 2, Montgomery County, Texas, ED 4, p. 2A, dwelling and family 28; digital image, *Ancestry.com* (http://ancestry.com : accessed 12 December 2010), citing National Archives and Records Administration microfilm T626, roll 2378. William and Mabel's youngest child is 15 years old in this census, putting William's death around 1915.

[107] 1930 U.S. census, Precinct 2, Montgomery County, Texas, ED 4, p. 2A, dwelling and family 28; digital image, *Ancestry.com* (http://ancestry.com : accessed 12 December 2010), citing National Archives and Records Administration microfilm T626, roll 2378.

[108] Texas Department of Health, State Vital Statistics Unit, "Texas Death Index, 1903-2000," database, *Ancestry.com* (http://search.ancestry.com : accessed 10 Dec 2010), entry for Mabel Mott.

[109] 1870 U.S. census, Pine Tavern District, Bullitt County, Kentucky, p. 28, dwelling 191, family 191, L.L.Owen; digital image, *Ancestry.com* (http://www.ancestry.com/ ; accessed 12 November 2010); citing National Archives and Records Administration microfilm M593, roll M593-450.

[110] 1850 U.S. census, District no. 2, Shelby County, Kentucky, p. 384 (verso); dwelling 658, family 675, Laura Owen; digital image, *Ancestry.com* (http://ancestry.com/ : accessed 28 November 2010) citing National Archives and Records Administration microfilm M432, roll 218.

[111] 1900 U.S. census, Kings, New York population schedule, Brooklyn, enumeration district (ED) 405; digital image, *Ancestry.com* (http://search.ancestry.com/cgi-bin/sse.dll?rank); citing National Archives and Records Administration microfilm T623, roll T623.

[112] 1900 U.S. census, Brooklyn, Kings County, New York, ED 405, sheet 2A, dwelling 25, family 27, Laura Mills; digital image, *Ancestry.com* (http://www.ancestry.com/ ; accessed 12 November 2010); citing National Archives and Records Administration microfilm T623, roll T623-1061. Isaac and Laura had been married for 30 years when the census taker came by. Mattie Lykins Bingham's bequest to "Mrs. Laura Mills of Brooklyn, a niece," tells us that the Laura who married Isaac C. Mills is the daughter of William Wooten Owen and Elizabeth Livingston. See "Bingham Gone," *Kansas City* (Missouri) *Times*, 4 November 1890, p. 1, cols. 5-6.

[113] 1900 U.S. census, Brooklyn, Kings County, New York, ED 405, sheet 2A, dwelling 25, family 27, Isaac Mills; digital image, *Ancestry.com* (http://www.ancestry.com/ ; accessed 12 November 2010); citing National Archives and Records Administration microfilm T623, roll T623-1061.

[114] 1900 U.S. census, Brooklyn, Kings County, New York, ED 405, sheet 2A, dwelling 25, family 27, Isaac Mills; digital image, *Ancestry.com* (http://www.ancestry.com/ ; accessed 12 November 2010); citing National Archives and Records Administration microfilm T623, roll T623-1061.

[115] 1900 U.S. census, Brooklyn, Kings County, New York, ED 405, sheet 2A, dwelling 25, family 27, May L. Mills; digital image, *Ancestry.com* (http://www.ancestry.com/ ; accessed 12 November 2010); citing National Archives and Records Administration microfilm T623, roll T623-1061.

[116] Ancestry.com, "Kentucky Birth Records, 1852-1910," np, Elizabeth Owen, digital image, *Ancestry.com* (http://ancestry.com/ : accessed 28 November 2010); citing Kentucky Department of Libraries and Archives microfilm set 994027-994058. See also Daughters of the American Revolution, "Descendants Database," *DAR Genealogical Research System* (http://services.dar.org/Public/DAR_Research/ : accessed 10 December 2010), Charlotte A. Ryder application, no. 164792, descendant of Brackett Owen. The applicant was the granddaughter of Elizabeth Livingston.

[117] Daughters of the American Revolution, "Descendants Database," *DAR Genealogical Research System* (http://services.dar.org/Public/DAR_Research/ : accessed 10 December 2010), Charlotte A. Ryder application, no. 164792, descendant of Brackett Owen. The applicant was the granddaughter of Elizabeth Livingston.

[118] Daughters of the American Revolution, "Descendants Database," *DAR Genealogical Research System* (http://services.dar.org/Public/DAR_Research/ : accessed 10 December 2010), Charlotte A. Ryder application, no. 164792, descendant of Brackett Owen. The applicant was the granddaughter of Elizabeth Livingston.

[119] 1880 U.S. census, Cumberland Central, Allegany, Maryland, ED 14, p. 12, dwelling 120, family 120, John A. Campbell; digital image, *Ancestry.com* (http://www.ancestry.com/ ; accessed 12 November 2010)*; citing National Archives and Records Administration microfilm T9, roll 494.

[120] Daughters of the American Revolution, "Descendants Database," *DAR Genealogical Research System* (http://services.dar.org/Public/DAR_Research/ : accessed 10 December 2010), Charlotte A. Ryder application, no. 164792, descendant of Brackett Owen. The applicant was the granddaughter of Elizabeth Livingston.

[121] 1880 U.S. census, Cumberland Central, Allegany, Maryland, ED 14, p. 12, dwelling 120, family 120, Lotta Campbell; digital image, *Ancestry.com* (http://www.ancestry.com/ ; accessed 12 November 2010); citing National Archives and Records Administration microfilm T9, roll 494.

[122] 1910 U.S. census, Pleasantville, Westchester County, New York, ED 50, sheet 8B, dwelling 161, family 178, Everett Ryder; digital image, *Ancestry.com* (http://www.ancestry.com/ : accessed 12 November 2010); citing National Archives and Records Administration microfilm T624, roll 1089. Everett and Charlotte had been married for 5 years when the census taker visited.

[123] 1920 U.S. census, Pleasantville, Westchester County, New York, ED 75, sheet 12A, dwelling 60, family 64, Everett Ryder; digital image, *Ancestry.com* (http://www.ancestry.com/ : accessed 12 November 2010); citing National Archives and Records Administration microfilm T625, roll 1276.

[124] 1870 U.S. census, Pine Tavern District, Bullitt County, Kentucky, p. 29, dwelling 199 and family 199, Dewit Owen; digital image, *Ancestry.com* (http://www.ancestry.com ; accessed 28 November 2010); citing National Archives and Records Administration microfilm M593, roll 593. See also Bureau of Vital Statistics, Missouri State Board of Health, Certificate of Death, file no. 38528, DeWitt Owen, 8 November 1939; digital image, Missouri State Archives, "Missouri Death Certificates, 1910-1960," Missouri Digital Heritage, Missouri Office of the Secretary of State (http://www.sos.mo.gov/mdh/ : accessed 8 December 2007).

[125] Bureau of Vital Statistics, Missouri State Board of Health, Certificate of Death, file no. 38528, DeWitt Owen, 8 November 1939; digital image, Missouri State Archives, "Missouri Death Certificates, 1910-1960," Missouri Digital Heritage, Missouri Office of the Secretary of State (http://www.sos.mo.gov/mdh/ : accessed 8 December 2007).

[126] Bureau of Vital Statistics, Missouri State Board of Health, Certificate of Death, file no. 38528, DeWitt Owen, 8 November 1939; digital image, Missouri State Archives, "Missouri Death Certificates, 1910-1960," Missouri Digital Heritage, Missouri Office of the Secretary of State (http://www.sos.mo.gov/mdh/ : accessed 8 December 2007).

[127] Recorder of Deeds, Jackson County, M issouri, Marriage License no. 24627, DeWitt Owen and Ada Campbell, 26 June 1902; digital image, Jackson County Recorder of Deeds (http://www.jacksongov.org : accessed 29 November 2010).

[128] 1885 Iowa State Census, Grant, Woodbury County, Iowa, p. 102, dwelling and family 94, Ada Campbell; online database, *Ancestry.com* (htpp://ancestry.com : accessed 8 Dec 2010). See also 1900 U.S. census, Esculapia Township, Benton County, Arkansas, ED 11, sheet 18-B, dwelling 379, family 395, Stephen Campbell family; digital image, *Ancestry.com* (http://www.ancestry.com ; accessed 28 November 2010); citing National Archives and Records Administration microfilm T623, roll 50. See also Robert Dewit Owen, New York to David W. Jackson, e-mail, 9 Feb 2011, "Mattie Lykins Bingham Genealogy"; privately held by Jackson.

[129] Social Security Administration, "Social Security Death Index," database, *Rootsweb.Ancestry.com* (http://www.rootsweb.ancestry.com : accessed 10 December 2010), entry for Ada Owen, SS no. 486-03-1355. See also Robert Dewit Owen, New York to David W. Jackson, e-mail, 9 Feb 2011, "Mattie Lykins Bingham Genealogy"; privately held by Jackson.

[130] Robert Dewit Owen, New York to David W. Jackson, e-mail, 9 Feb 2011, "Mattie Lykins Bingham Genealogy"; privately held by Jackson.

[131] Robert Dewit Owen, New York to David W. Jackson, e-mail, 9 Feb 2011, "Mattie Lykins Bingham Genealogy"; privately held by Jackson.

[132] 1870 U.S. census, Pine Tavern District, Bullitt County, Kentucky, p. 28, dwelling and family 191, William Owen; digital image, *Ancestry.com* (http://www..ancestry.com/ : accessed 19 November 2010); citing National Archives and Records Administration microfilm M593, roll 450.

[133] 1930 U.S. census, Precinct 2, Montgomery County, Texas, ED 4, p. 2A, dwelling and family 28; digital image, *Ancestry.com* (http://www.ancestry.com : accessed 12 December 2010), citing National Archives and Records Administration microfilm T626, roll 2378. William and Mabel's youngest child is 15 years old in this census, putting William's death around 1915.

[134] 1930 U.S. census, Precinct 2, Montgomery County, Texas, ED 4, p. 2A, dwelling and family 28; digital image, *Ancestry.com* (http://www.ancestry.com : accessed 12 December 2010), citing National Archives and Records Administration microfilm T626, roll 2378.

[135] Texas Department of Health, State Vital Statistics Unit, "Texas Death Index, 1903-2000," database, *Ancestry.com* (http://www.ancestry.com : accessed 10 Dec 2010), entry for Mabel Mott.

[136] 1920 U.S. census, Justice Precinct 4, Harris County, Texas, ED 114, sheet 16-B, dwelling 365, family 383; dital image, *Ancestry.com* (http://www.ancestry.com : accessed 10 December 2010).

[137] 1920 U.S. census, Justice Precinct 4, Harris County, Texas, ED 114, sheet 16-B, dwelling 365, family 383; dital image, *Ancestry.com* (http://www.ancestry.com : accessed 10 December 2010).

[138] 1880 U.S. census, Cumberland Central, Allegany, Maryland, ED 14, p. 12, dwelling 120, family 120, Lotta Campbell; digital image, *Ancestry.com* (http://www.ancestry.com/ ; accessed 12 November 2010); citing National Archives and Records Administration microfilm T9, roll 494.

[139] 1920 U.S. census, Pleasantville, Westchester County, New York, ED 75, p. 12A, ; digital image, *Ancestry.com* (http://www..ancestry.com : accessed 29 November 2010), citing National Archives and Records Administration microfilm T625, roll T625-1276.

[140] Social Security Administration, "Social Security Death Index," database, Rootsweb.*Ancestry.com* (http://www..ancestry.com : accessed 27 Nov 2010), entry for Everett O. Ryder, SS no. 164-10-7101. See also 1910 U.S. census, Pleasantville, Westchester County, New York, ED 50, sheet 8-B, dwelling 161, family 178, Ryder family; digital image, *Ancestry.com* (http://www.ancestry.com : accessed 29 November 2010).

[141] Social Security Administration, "Social Security Death Index," database, Rootsweb.*Ancestry.com* (http://www..ancestry.com : accessed 27 Nov 2010), entry for Everett O. Ryder, SS no. 164-10-7101

[142] Robert Dewit Owen, New York to David W. Jackson, e-mail, 9 Feb 2011, "Mattie Lykins Bingham Genealogy"; privately held by Jackson.

[143] Robert Dewit Owen, New York to David W. Jackson, e-mail, 9 Feb 2011, "Mattie Lykins Bingham Genealogy"; privately held by Jackson.

[144] Robert Dewit Owen, New York to David W. Jackson, e-mail, 9 Feb 2011, "Mattie Lykins Bingham Genealogy"; privately held by Jackson.

[145] Robert Dewit, New York to David W. Jackson, e-mail, 9 Feb 2011, "Mattie Lykins Bingham Genealogy"; privately held by Jackson.

[146] Robert Dewit Owen, New York to David W. Jackson, e-mail, 9 Feb 2011, "Mattie Lykins Bingham Genealogy"; privately held by Jackson.

[147] Robert Dewit Owen, New York to David W. Jackson, e-mail, 9 Feb 2011, "Mattie Lykins Bingham Genealogy"; privately held by Jackson.

Recollections of Old Times in Kansas City

By Martha Ann "Mattie" (Livingston) Lykins Bingham

The following is a faithful transcription of an undated, 67-page, handwritten recollection written by Mrs. Martha Ann "Mattie" (Livingston) Lykins Bingham. Mattie married Dr. Johnston Lykins in 1851. Dr. Lykins died August 15, 1876. Mrs. Lykins married General George Caleb Bingham on June 18, 1878, at the Lykins Institute, where Mrs. Lykins served as proprietress. General Bingham died the following year.

The cover of the *American Blotter Writing Tablet* bears a copyright date of 1883 by the Acme Stationery and Paper Company, New York. This recollection was thus written between 1883 and September 20, 1890, when Mrs. Bingham died at The Washington Hotel at 12th and Washington, Kansas City, Missouri.

This recollection, in a leather satchel, was among Mrs. Bingham's belongings, and it had been preserved in the family for many years. Dewit Livingston Owen acquired the manuscript after Mrs. Bingham died. Mrs. Ada Owen maintained it after her husband died in 1939. Robert Dewit Owen inherited his grandmother's papers upon her death in July 1971. Among those materials was Mrs. Bingham's original recollection.

This and four other unpublished manuscripts by Ada Owen (and a photograph of Caleb Bingham) were donated to the Jackson County Historical Society, Independence, Missouri, in August 2009, by Robert Dewit Owen, in memory of his grandmother, Mrs. Dewit Livingston (Ada Armintha Campbell) Owen, an early member and supporter of the Jackson County Historical Society. In March 2011, Mr. Owen generously added to this collection an original 1865 ambrotype of Martha Ann "Mattie" (Livingston) Lykins that debuts in this biography, *Missouri Star:*

In turning back the pages of memory to the first years of my life spent in this city, I find dates, and even well known localities almost obliterated by time. After spending the winter of 1851 and 1852 in Washington City with my husband, Dr. J[ohnston] Lykins, we landed in Kansas City the first week in March 1852. The boat on which we had taken passage at St. Louis, was the second one to reach our wharf that spring. In those days the arrival of the first steamboats of the season was generally hailed with delight and usually brought to the levee, every man and boy in our town.

For the three winter months of the year we were locked in from the busy world by ice and snow, hence the opening of navigation was recognized as the key that unlocked the door to commercial life and activity.

At that time, Kansas City could hardly be called even a village. It was better known as Westport Landing, grouped along the levee were a few cheaply constructed warehouses and two or three stores which consisted of a mixed stock of goods. This meant everything from calico and silk down to groceries, hardware, tinware, ready made clothing and shoes for man and beast. We had one little drug store that dealt chiefly in quinine and patent medicines. In this little ten by fifteen foot room, our worthy postmaster found quarters for himself, and an old goods box with less than a dozen pigeon holes in it for the reception and safe keeping of our once-a-week mail. A shoe mending shop, several saloons and the Gillis House about comprised the entire list of buildings on the levee.

On the high bluff, overlooking the river were two or three comfortable brick dwellings. Scattered farther back from the bluff was a wagon and blacksmith's shop, a small boarding house and a few one-story log and frame buildings. These, so far as my recollection goes, about covered the extent of the improvements on the hill. Not a street was cut through the bluff to the river. Vehicles of all kinds, in order to reach the buildings on the bluff, had to follow a road that led down the river a short distance, then it turned abruptly at the foot of the bluff into an ungraded street where Grand Avenue now starts from the river. This road was followed a few yards south, then it again turned and [ran] diagonally across some vacant lots into what is now Main Street, by a circuitous route. This road [ran] *south to Westport, crossing O.K.* [Creek] *a little west of the bridge that now spans the creek. At that time we considered O.K. Creek quite a stream. It often afforded us a good mess of little fish for breakfast which we esteemed a real treat.*

The first baptism by emersion that ever occurred in Kansas City (so far as I know) took place in this creek. Just at the crossing of the creek a deep pool of water had formed, and near the bank lived a very clever family in a log house. In this house the candidates for baptism dressed and walked to the creek, returning to the same house to change their clothes after the baptism. One Sabbath afternoon shortly after a baptism had taken place, a heavy rain came up which swelled the creek into a wide and rapid stream. A hack that plied daily between this city and Westport, chanced that afternoon to be caught on this side of the creek. After waiting an hour or two for the water to subside, the driver becoming impatient, decided to cross the stream. The horses had no sooner struck the current than they were lifted off their feet. The hack was overturned and the horses and two passengers in the hack were drowned.

In 1852 the Indians roamed our streets in all their native freedom and often without the least fear of disturbance, they slept in the tall weeds and hazel brush that grew on our hills in patches. In the month of December our farmers generally killed their hogs and sold to us our year's meat which we cut up and salted away without ever a thought of such an enemy to human life as [trichinosis]. *Usually about hog killing time and during the ripening of the different kinds of wild fruits that grew abundantly with us, the Indians were our most frequent and troublesome visitors. The first year of my housekeeping, I well remember one morning in December, just as I was about to leave my room for the kitchen to superintend the making of our sausage meat and head cheese. I was called hastily to see a neighbor's child, which hat at that moment met with a serious accident. On my return home, I found our kitchen in possession of ten or fifteen Indians* [sic.] *braves with as many squaws and papooses. Not a living soul was to be seen about the premises, save the loud talking Indians. Two or three squaws had contentedly seated themselves before the fire and were cooking pieces of meat tied to the end*

151

of long sticks while their companions were examining the contents of our kitchen cupboard. Suddenly they discovered me entering the back porch and with one bound the whole band rushed towards me wildly gesticulating and by every sign they could invent tried to tell me that something had happened which they wanted to explain. I confess I was badly frightened and hardly knew whether to stand my ground or to seek protection at one of our neighbors. However, I mustered up sufficient courage to stamp my foot quite vigorously and at the same time I pointed toward the yard gate as a command for them to leave. They evidently mistook my meaning and thought I meant to tell them that they had driven our servants off through the yard gate. Immediately a big, dirty, tough looking Indian brave caught me by the arm and more dragging than leading me, ran towards the stable that stood on the rear part of the lot. Laughing immoderately, he pointed towards the upper part of the stable from which I understood that our servants had taken refuge there. At once, I loudly called our woman servant by name. She silently responded by showing her face at a window in the loft. The colored boy then grew bold and thrust his inky head out at another opening in the stable. Assuring them there was really no harm in the Indians, I bade them come down and go back to their work. With due alacrity and generosity, I filled their sacks with hog's heads and meat, after which they left without ceremony. The following winter the same band returned and I traded them meat and flour for parched squaw corn and hominy. During the summer and fall months we depended chiefly on the Indians for our fruit and berries for preserving. It seemed to afford them pleasure to bring to our doors, on their ponies, nice baskets of wild strawberries, blackberries, gooseberries, grapes, plums and wild crab apples thickly covered over with paw-paw leaves to protect them from the heat of the sun. Among the many other good services they rendered us, they kept our tables supplied bountifully with the best of dried buffalo meat and with a kind of parched corn, which when cooked, was delicious enough for the gods to eat.

In those days, wild game was abundant. It was nothing unusual for prairie chickens in their flight from one field to another to light on the trees in our yard for rest. Flocks of quails in search for food would often come trooping into our gardens chattering their bird talk as fearlessly as if no man was near to dispute their right to the earth under their feet. When discovered, and hard pressed by boys or dogs, they did not hesitate to seek safety in our houses. I have often caught them in my room under the sofa or bed and set them free that they might live to come again.

Herds of buffalo were often seen on the prairie a few miles south of Westport cropping the tall grass without the least fear of a stray shot or the huntsman's lasso. Even in these early days our village at the mouth of the Kaw was a stirring, bustling, busy place.

In the Spring, just as early as the grass was sufficiently advanced to sustain life in oxen and mules, the loud whoop and the sharp crack of the unmerciful whip of Mexican peons and greasers could be heard from dawn until midnight. This point on the Missouri river certainly seemed destined by the hand of nature to be the great depot for all kinds of supplies for New Mexico and the Indian country. It was also the outfitting station and starting point for emigrants to California and Salt Lake City. I have known thousands of Mormons to be landed here in one season. Like weary cattle after a long drive, they pitched their tents over our hills for rest and recuperation before starting across the plains to the promised land of their hopes and faith. Poor things; discouraged, sick and feeble from their long sea and river voyage, many laid down in their tents never to rise again. To add to their afflictions, notwithstanding, they were warned by our citizens, they cooked and ate poisonous weeds, from the effects of which many died the victims of their own folly and ignorance.

Our town then numbered in population less than three hundred, whites, negroes and Indians all told. Our only official guardian was a township marshall who was rarely to be found when needed. A little log Catholic church presided over by Father Donnelly, was the only place of worship nearer than Westport or Independence. We had no newspapers, school houses, telegraph lines, market hours, butcher's shops, bakeries, milliner's shop or dressmaking establishments to worry our brains or to drain our pocketbooks.

The latest fashions in dress, parties, luncheons, receptions, operas and the modern club houses with their luxurious trappings did not in the least disturb the quiet of our homes. We lived in blissful ignorance of such pleasures, yet, strange to say, we were a happy and contented people. We wore our ginghams, lawns and calicoes to our best entertainments and a pretty shaker or white corded sunbonnet was the pride of our life. True, we had better gowns and bonnets but they were worn only on rare occasions.

The first Protestant church built in our city was commenced in the summer of 1852. While the erection of the church was under the auspices of the Methodist denomination, yet it was understood by all who contributed to the building fund that it was to be used on alternated Sundays by any denomination that chose to occupy it. The first summer it was commenced our citizens succeeded in getting it roofed in and windows and doors in. The following summer it was plastered, but there was no means of heating, or lighting the building. The ladies now felt that the time had come for them to put their shoulders to the wheel and aid in providing means for lighting and warming the church. With this purpose in view, we got together on one day's notice and organized a sewing society with the intention of holding a fair in the church building in the early part of the fall. On Thursday afternoon of each week, we met at the residence of some member of the society and our fingers flew for dear life until six o'clock when we were served with a bountiful and elegant supper. In the early part of September of that year, I was called to Louisville, Kentucky. Having been elected President of the society at the organization, I called the ladies together before leaving and urged them to meet as usual every week during my absence and to be ready to hold their fair about the middle of October when I hoped to with then again. I was unavoidably detained in Kentucky and did not return until the 8th of December.

A few weeks before leaving Louisville for home, I received a letter from the secretary of our society telling me the ladies had only met once since I left. At that meeting they did not seem to know how to conduct the affairs of the society so without a dissenting voice decided not to meet until I returned. In view of this discouraging report, I concluded our fair project would prove a failure. However, before leaving Louisville, I decided to purchase a few articles suitable for a fair which proved to be a wise and profitable investment. That year our winter set in very early and with unusual severity. After the middle of November, but few steamboats were willing to leave St. Louis for the Upper Missouri river. But luckily for us, a few days after we reached St. Louis, one captain was courageous enough to raise stream for Kansas City. On this boat we took passage for home. All went well until we entered the Missouri river. Here we encountered floating ice which increased in quantity and thickness until the wheels of our boat were powerless to make a revolution. At the little town of Cambridge, we were put ashore and our boat overturned to St. Louis by floating with the ice, guided by the pilot to keep her in the current. At Cambridge, we hired a private conveyance and after two or three days of hard travel over rough, frozen roads, we landed at home, sore in every limb and utterly worn our with fatigue. I had scarcely thrown off my heavy wraps when the door of our sitting room burst open and every member of our sewing society rushed in to greet me. Tired as I was, before they left we had pluckily decided to hold our fair on Christmas Eve and it was then the 8th of December. But where and in what building were questions we had not stopped to consider. The thermometer was then below zero, so we could not think of holding it in the church. People would freeze and such a thing as the need of a public hall had never entered the head of our most enterprising citizen, so we had none. While throwing off my wraps I had noticed from a window in my room that a steamboat lay tied up at our wharf which had been caught at this point by the heavy ice. I asked the ladies the name of the unlucky boat. On being informed, I was glad to remember the name of the captain as an old acquaintance. Knowing his address to be Booneville, [Missouri], it occurred to me that it would not be amiss to drop him a line and ask him for the use of his boat for our fair. Hardly hoping for a favorable reply, that night before retiring I mailed a letter to him. Sooner than I had expected, a reply came and such a genuine surprise as it was. It dispelled every cloud of anxiety and removed every obstacle in the way of our fair. In his letter to me, he enclosed one to the man left in charge of the boat, directing him to place

155

at our service that boat with its kitchen, cooking utensils, stoves, china, silver, and table linen, and to render us all the assistance he could in arranging for our fair. With this unexpected streak of good luck, you may readily imagine we held our fair as we had planned on the evening of Dec 24*th*.

On the following evening at the same place, we gave a children's party. These two entertainments netted our society $500. With a population of less than four hundred, I venture to say that no fair held since in our city in proportion to population has ever excelled in its receipts the first fair ~~ever~~ held in Kansas City. To the trustees of the church we turned over the $500 which warmed, lighted and carpeted the first Protestant church ever erected in Kansas City. During the summer of 1854 it was dedicated to the worship of the Most Holy One, but today, I am pained to say that it is used for a livery stable and its walls are made to echo every hour with words of profanity that falls from the lips of those for whom it was built to save from the wrath to come. Our first Sunday school was organized and held in this church before it was finished.

The Rev. Nathan Scarritt, now living in the eastern part of the city, was then a young active Methodist minister in charge of a circuit that embraced Kansas City. On one of his ministerial rounds he called to see Dr. Lykins and myself in reference to organizing a Sunday school Dr. Lykins warmly favored the school but told him that his professional duties would not permit him to perform the duties of [superintendent]. As a result of Mr. Scarritt's visit, the school was organized and I had to fill the place of teacher and superintendent.

At first, we had rather a disorderly set to deal with, but we managed to come out all right. The first Sunday our school opened five or six rough looking boys entered the church and took their seats near the door evidently intending to run things to suit themselves. I kindly invited them to join our school but they rudely declined. Very soon two or three of the gang began to shoot wet wads of paper against the walls and the ceiling, while others purposely let fall some marbles which rattled their way down the entire length of the floor. They spit tobacco in every direction and drew pictures on the pews with chalk and provokingly laughed out aloud. I repeatedly remonstrated with them, but my words only seemed to make them more determined to keep up their annoyance. The next Sunday morning when I entered the church they stood congregated outside. I spoke to them politely but they did not return my salutation. Immediately after school opened they entered the church and again seated themselves near the door. This time they had brought with them under ~~the~~ cover of their coats, two cats, these they placed on the seat beside them, which they soon teased into a terrific fight. I requested them to turn the cats out and to desist from further disturbing the school. But they paid no attention to my request. At last I felt their conduct had reached a point where forbearance ceased to be a virtue. I was in the midst of hearing my Bible class when the tortured and teased cats again engaged in a furious fight. I quietly laid down my book and walked up to the door and put the cats out, then I turned to the boys and read them a lecture which had the desired effect. From that moment they remained perfectly quiet until the school closed. The third Sunday morning they were in their usual seats near the door. Before opening the school I approached them and offering them my hand in token of forgiveness for their past conduct, I asked them if they were not now ready to join in our school and to be good boys in the future. To my amazement, without the least hesitation they assented. I invited them to take seats nearer the few classes we had which they kindly did. On handing each one a book, to my astonishment I found only one of the number could read. This Sunday saw the end of our Sunday school trouble. The boys soon grew to love their teachers and school and ever after that day they rivaled in good conduct and politeness the best scholars we had.

Just here I would like to say that the question has repeatedly been asked me, "How did you manage to spend your time in those days?" "Your society must have been very much mixed and at a fearfully low ebb both morally and intellectually." I have invariably replied that our society was not as much mixed then as now. True the circle of our best society was not so extensive but as far as it went, it would be hard to find in our city today, a more intelligent, refined and cultured class of ladies. More than this, they found time to be practical and without the aid of our modern conveniences. In their homes, were

157

models of neatness and good order. Their children were never neglected but at all times they were well dressed and well behaved. And be it said to their credit that every stitch in their well made garments was put in by the fingers of their patient and devoted mothers. Not a sewing machine had then crossed the Mississippi river and not a woman lived in our town that had to earn her bread by the needle. No village gossip, no tales or scandal, no divorce suits and no church or neighborhood quarrels ever disturbed the quiet of our social and domestic life. Neither was any woman of an unsavory reputation or one suspected of being unfaithful to her marriage vows ever permitted to enter the "charmed circle of our best society." Money, fine clothes, fine equipages and servants in livery had no value when compared to virtue and gentle breeding and a character above reproach. The refined, pure and primitive simplicity that adorned the domestic and social life of our ladies in those days would reflect no discredit on the ladies of the present age, but would rather tend to throw around their homes a halo of happiness and contentment unknown to many elegant homes and families at the present time.

But to return to my recollections of old times in Kansas City.

As a matter of history, it is known to you that during the winter of 1852 and 1853, congress entered into a treaty with the Indian tribes on our border which brought into existence the State of Kansas and led to what is known as the Border War. Up to that time, we had slept with our doors unlocked and with our money in keyless drawers.

We had neither banks nor vaults, nor did we need them. Not that gold and silver were strangers to us, we had plenty of both, but we coveted no man's wealth enough to steal it. However, the tide of emigration that set in upon us after the treaty, brought with it thieves and murderers from every part of our globe. In the struggle that followed the treaty between the political parties to gain possession of Kansas, the North and South soon became arrayed against each other in deadly strife. Men went around armed and life was unsafe. Doors had to be locked and money had to seek a safe hiding place. Boats on landing to discharge their cargoes were taken possession of and searched for arms and ammunition. Old John Brown who had enjoyed the freedom of our town was no longer permitted to show himself on our streets. Reason was dethroned and passion and prejudice drove men to commit deeds of cruelty and injustice which would have shocked their sense of right and humanity under other circumstances. Thus the war raged until General Reeder who had been appointed by the President, Governor of Kansas, was forced to flee for his life from the territory.

Well do I remember the night of his flight to Kansas City and his place of concealment here for several weeks. A number of young, hot-headed southerners had organized themselves into a military company for the purpose of preventing settlers from entering Kansas. This self organized and indiscreet company determined to intercept Governor Reeder and capture him if possible. They had ~~very~~ rightly supposed that he would make his way to Kansas City through some secret channel and from this point would make his escape by boat to St. Louis. In order to cut off his retreat and to effect his capture they stationed pickets on the levee and searched every boat that landed at our wharf from the Upper Missouri. Col[onel] Coates [Kersey], Dr. Lykins and Mr. Eldridge of the Eldridge House, afterwards known at the Gillis Hotel, were the only gentlemen in our city who were informed in reference to his movements. They had purposely delayed his coming to Kansas City as long as they could with the hope that the excitement then existing might abate.

However, he was so hotly pressed by his enemies in the rear that his friends finally decided that it would not be safe to longer postpone his escape from Kansas. Hence, it was arranged that on a certain night a skiff should be sent up the river by a trusty man to a designated point where Gov[ernor] Reeder would be in waiting. In the meantime, the men who had been standing guard for so many long hot days and nights had really relaxed in vigilance and greatly reduced the number of pickets. Fortunately the night Gov[ernor] Reeder was expected, there was but one picket on duty. The remainder of the company had retired for the night to a room used as headquarters in a building on the corner of Main Street and the Levee.

Between one and two o'clock that night, under the shelter of a starless sky, this lone picket was startled by the dipping of oars and the splashing of water. Looking in the direction from whence the sound came, he discovered a skiff near the shore with two men on it. With one *strong stroke of the oarsman, the boat touched the shore. The large[r] man of the two, sprang out and walked rapidly towards the hotel, the door in the basement swung open and he entered without a word being spoken, or the fall of a footstep being heard. The man left the skiff without heeding the command of the picket to halt, struck out in the middle of the stream and was soon lost to sight. The picket was sorely puzzled to account for the maneuvers of the men. After a moment's reflection it occurred to him that the man who had left the skiff and entered the hotel so quietly might possibly be Gov[ernor] Reeder. He hastened to headquarters and imparted his suspicions to his comrades. He urged them to go with him and guard the hotel until morning when they could search the house for the stranger. But the men were too drunk and heavy with stupor to heed his entreaties. They declared they knew the men in the skiff to be negro chicken thieves who had been out on a marauding expedition. Thoroughly disgusted with his comrades in arms, the picket seated himself on a goods box near the door of headquarters and there rested until the sun had risen some distance above the horizon the next morning.*

This lone picket was none other than Mr. Alexander Lawton of Georgia after whom Lawton's Addition in this city is named. He was a cultured and refined gentleman but an ardent southerner in sympathy and politics. Feeling the need of a good hot cup of coffee after his night of picket duty, he rang our front door bell just as we had seated ourselves at the breakfast table. He was kindly invited out to the breakfast room and while enjoying his cup of coffee, he related what had taken place on the levee during the night. He further expressed it as his belief that the man who had entered the house was none other than Gov[ernor] Reeder and so strong were his convictions of this, he said he meant to have the hotel searched from cellar to garret during the day. As we knew it had been planned for Gov[ernor] Reeder to come to our city that night by skiff, we felt quite sure that Mr. Lawton was not mistaken in his surmises. Dr. Lykins manifested no particular concern about the story while Mr. Lawton was relating it but hurriedly eating his breakfast asked to be excused giving as a reason that he had several very sick patients to see. He was not long in reaching the Eldridge House and in imparting to

160

Col[onel] Coates and Mr. Eldridge the information he had gained from Mr. Lawton. At once, they took steps to remove Gov[ernor] Reeder to a place of safety. True to his word in the afternoon of the same day, Mr. Lawton had the Eldridge House searched from cellar to garret, but the bird was not in the cage. The place of concealment selected for Gov. Reeder was in the loft of an old house which stood on a hill west of Broadway. It was perfectly obscured by thick hazel brush, paw-paw trees and wild grape vines. During his confinement I often sent him nice things to eat and conveyed to him weekly, clean handkerchiefs and changes of underwear. The torture of suspense and the want of outdoor exercise affected his health and he was soon confined to his cot by nervous prostration and fever.

When it was absolutely necessary for Dr. Lykins to visit him professionally, in order to elude suspicion he would have the wife of the old man who lived in the house to feign sickness and send for hm. As his ill health was really caused by anxiety and close confinement he daily grew weaker and more impatient to be free. His friends realizing that his life depended on his release from confinement planned for his escape on a boat as a wood chopper, which as a matter of history is too well known to be of interest here. Suffice it is to say that in the course of time hostilities ceased and we were once more a happy and prosperous people.

But alas! Our peace and prosperity was of short duration. In a few short years we were again plunged into another war between the North and South more terrible than ever. It is not my purpose here to discuss the right or wrong of that dreadful conflict, nor to drag from the grave of the past the bitter, lingering remembrances of those sad days. But we should forever bear in remembrance the time when our fields were ruined and our homes desolated. The anguish of broken hearts, the cries of the widow and fatherless, the pain and suffering of the crippled and maimed on both sides as an indelible warning on the pages of memory never again to resort to the sword and torch as the arbitrators of our sectional disputes. Often during the war it really seemed to me that Kansas City got more than her share of the bitterness of the strife. The daily tread of thousands of soldiers in our streets, the alarming reports of the invasion of our state by the Confederate army, the harrowing

161

telegraphic dispatches of the dreadful slaughter of the contending armies, the harassing and daily warfare carried on in our county between the Kansas Jayhawkers and the Missouri Bushwhackers kept us in a state of alarm and excitement for four years without a day's intermission.

But the many stirring and thrilling incidents of the war, none brought to our very door more sadness and desolation than the sacking of Lawrence and the enforcement of Order No. 11. I would not here allude to this particular and painful event of the war, but for the fact that I was an eye witness to the Lawrence Massacre and to the rigid enforcement of Order No.11, hence, without the slightest desire to extenuate the one or to condemn the other, I feel that in the name of history I have the right to speak of what I know to be the facts connected with that tragic event.

It was only a few weeks ago that I read a notice in one of our morning papers of a meeting held in this city by the "George H. Tomas Post" of the G.A.R. at the corner of 11th and Main Streets, at which a gentleman read a paper on the "Lawrence Massacre" in which he characterized Order No.11 "as just, humane and deserved." He doubtless said what he believed to be true but he evidently was not informed as to the real facts that led to the Lawrence Massacre, which under no circumstances and for nor provocation on earth ought ever to have taken place. But the spirit of retaliation is subject to no law and excuses governed by right or reason.

In seeking revenge, too often the innocent and not the guilty are made to drink to the very dregs the bitterness of man's inhumanity to man. Now, I beg to repeat that my sole purpose in alluding to the Lawrence Massacre in this paper is simply to throw a little light on the cause which I believe led to it and which, so far as I know, has never reached the ear of the public through the press or through any other medium. It is doubtless known to all before me as a matter of history, that during the war many southern women were arrested and imprisoned on suspicion of aiding and abetting the Confederate cause. As a place of imprisonment for such in this city, an old dilapidated brick building on the levee once known and used as the Mechanics Bank, was taken possession of by the military authorities and set apart as a prison for Rebel women. After the building had been occupied as such for some

162

time it became so infested with rats and vermin of all kinds as to render it unfit for human beings to live in. Even the health of the guards, who had access to the river for bathing, suffered so much from the stench and torture of the vermin as to lead them to appeal to headquarters for a change of location. According to their request, a building was selected which stood about the middle of a block of brick buildings known as the Metropolitan Block on Grand Avenue between 13th and 14th Streets. The house selected belonged to General Bingham [George Caleb Bingham] who at that time was treasurer of the state and living in Jeff[erson City, Missouri]. For more than six years previous to the war, General Bingham had lived in Europe. The death of several near relatives led him to return to this country with some large paintings unfinished which he had been commissioned by the legislature of this state to paint for the capitol building at Jeff City. For the purposed of finishing these large paintings it was necessary for him to have a studio with light unobstructed by surrounding objects. Hence, some months before he left Europe, he wrote to a party in this city to have a competent architect examine his building in the Metropolitan Block on Grand Avenue and if thought to be strong enough to bear the weight of an additional story twenty feet high to have the story added to the building. The opinion of the architect being favorable, it was ready for General Bingham on his return. He continued to occupy the building both as a studio and residence until appointed by President Lincoln, treasurer of the state, which office had suddenly been made vacant by the flight of Gov[ernor] [Claiborne] Jackson and his cabinet to the Confederate States. General Thomas Ewing was then in command of this military district with headquarters at Kansas City. He did not notify General Bingham that his building was needed for a prison, but simply took possession of it and ordered the women prisoners transferred to it and confined in the third story which General Bingham had used for his studio. The Metropolitan Block was so constructed that the sleepers [horizontal beams] of the floors served the purpose of braces to the dividing walls of each building. The sleepers of the first floor rested on brick pillars in the cellar. In the exciting events of the times our citizens had forgotten the imprisoned women until one hot day, Friday, August 14th, about two o'clock, this prison fell, burying beneath its walls a number of its inmates, four of whom were dreadfully mangled and crushed to death. Others had limbs broken or dislocated. I was told that on investigation it was learned (and I think this testimony may be found on file in the Claim Department of the War office in Washington City), that the building had been weakened by the removal of the brick pillars which supported the first floor, and further that some of the sleepers of the adjoining buildings on both sides had also been removed, thus weakening the dividing walls beyond safety. By whom this inhuman act was done, was not known, for what purpose, was left to conjecture. In less than an hour after this building fell, I was informed by some of the women prisoners that they had repeatedly been told by their guards that the house was giving away and would eventually fall. "But," they said, "We had so often been told during our imprisonment, equally as alarming stories which proved false, that we paid no attention to this one, yet, every few days we heard the building crack, which was invariably followed by the falling of pieces of plastering from the ceiling."

Dr. Joshua Thorne, who still lives in our City, was at that time chief surgeon of the hospital at this place. While I stood beside him, near the building, watching the removal of the living and the dead from the debris, some one remarked to him that they supposed some of the soldiers on guard would be found buried beneath the ruins. "No," replied Dr. Thorne, "Not a blue coat will be found; every man who has been detailed to stand guard at this prison for the last few weeks, knew the house to be unsafe and have kept themselves at a safe distance from the trembling walls. I knew the building to be unsafe," he continued, "and notified the military authorities of the fact, and suggested the removal of the women prisoners, but my suggestion was not heeded. Before you is the result."

Of course, the truth was not only told in reference to the sad affair, but the most exaggerated reports went over the country to the relatives and friends of the dead and crippled women prisoners, which naturally aroused the most terrible feelings of revenge among the men who had sworn allegiance to the Southern Confederacy. On the following Friday morning, August 21st, about sunrise, Quantrell [sic.], with five hundred men entered Lawrence. It was my misfortune to be in Lawrence on that eventful morning.

From the plating [sic.] out of Lawrence, it had been the home of my step-son, W[illiam] H. R. Lykins. I had not [paid] him and his family a visit for over three years. The day before the ~~falling of the~~ prison fell, I chanced to write to his wife that I would be in Lawrence on the following Monday. Never for one moment suspecting danger, I left home in the [sic.] for Lawrence early on Monday morning taking with me Col[onel] Case's little three year old daughter.

As I remember now, it was as late as five or six o'clock in the afternoon before we reached Lawrence. After bathing my face and hands and resting awhile, I joined the family on the front porch. I asked my step-son, as I took my seat, what was the news in Lawrence. "We have the best of news," he replied. "The commander of Fort Leavenworth notified us last week that Quantrell and his band had left the border of Missouri and had gone South. On the strength of this authentic information, he added, we were ordered to stack our arms in the arsenal and to go home and sleep the sleep of peace and security. We have had a hard time of it this summer," he added. "We have stood guard every night for months and we were beginning to feel pretty well used up for want of rest from drill and guard duties." I replied that I was "glad to hear from so reliable a source that Quantrell and his band had gone South and hoped they would remain there."

During the run of our conversation, I told him of the falling of the Rebel prison and the death of four women as the result. He said he had not heard of it, which did not surprise me in the least as no mention of the sad occurrence had been made in any of the papers of our city.

That evening before retiring for the night, I heard continuous firing for several minutes. As my son had just informed me that the citizens had been ordered to stack their guns in the arsenal, I did not know what the firing meant, so I asked the cause of it. He said, "Col. Jennison is raising a new regiment called the Kansas 17th and a few recruits of this regiment are encamped near the town, to avoid the heat of the day they usually drill early in the morning or late in the evening and are in the habit of firing off their guns after the drill."

165

It so happened the morning Quantrell entered Lawrence that I got up to lower the window shades in my room, just as the morning sun was beginning to redden the eastern horizon. A view of the entire town with the beautiful prairie surrounding it lay before me like a lovely picture. All was as quiet and peaceful as though the roar of the cannon had never been heard in our land. I had scarcely laid down again, when I heard rapid firing. My bed stood near a window from which a good view of the town and prairie could be had. Leaning over the foot of my bed I drew the curtain aside and looked out in the direction of the firing. I saw a number of horsemen riding to and fro and could plainly see the smoke from their guns.

Without the slightest suspicion of what was transpiring I sat up in bed and watched them until the firing ceased. After which they fell into line four abreast and rode rapidly down Massachusetts St., to the Eldridge House where they halted. In a few moments, a white sheet floated from one of the windows which I took to be the work of a chambermaid cleaning up rooms, but it proved to be a flag of truce unfurled by the Provo Marshall of the State who chanced to be in the hotel. In an instant after this, the horsemen spread over the town in every direction. Just as they broke ranks, a laboring man came jogging along riding one horse and leading another, when within a few yards of meeting the guerillas he seemed suddenly to discover that they were enemies. Dropping the reins of the horse he was leading, he fled for dear life in an opposite direction. This convinced me that all was not right. I immediately woke up Mrs. Lykins, [Mattie's daughter-in-law] *who was soundly sleeping with her baby beside her, only a few weeks old. I told her to hurry and get up, that the town was full of armed men riding in every direction and I could not tell what it meant. More asleep than awake she slowly got up and rubbing her eyes, looked out and said, "Oh! Those fellows belong to Jennison's regiment. They are just riding about in the cool of the morning for fun." As she turned to lay down again, I saw a workman in his shirt sleeves and with a pipe in his mouth approaching the foundation of a new building near by. He was within a few paces of the house before he discovered the guerrillas. Instantly, he rushed towards the building and without heeding their command to halt, with one bound landed in the basement. I saw them level their guns and with unerring aim they shot him dead. Mr. Lykins, [William H. R.] who was sleeping in another room, was about the last member of his family to be made acquainted with the appalling situation. Throwing on his clothes he started for the door with the hope of making his escape to a cornfield near by. By this time the guerillas had surrounded his house and were guarding every avenue of escape. I told him that escape was impossible and that his safety depended on his remaining in the house. Still, he insisted on making the attempt, fearing he would do so, with all the physical strength I had, I held him back and by dint force and argument succeeded in getting him back into his room. I then locked the door and put the key in my pocket. It was thus that he escaped death. Four or five days after the Lawrence Massacre, General Ewing issued his famous Order No. 11, which led to as much destruction of property by pillage and the torch and almost as great a number of innocent lives as Quantrell's raid had inflicted upon poor ill-fated Lawrence.*

Sometime after my return from Lawrence I was creditably informed, (at least I thought so then and have had no reason to change my mind) that Quantrell immediately on hearing of the death of the women, (all of whom were either wives or sisters of his men), called a council of war and it was decided that he should address a note to the commander at this place and demand the release of the women who had escaped death instead of sending them to Gratiot Prison in St. Louis as they had heard he meant to do, and to further say that if their request was not immediately complied with, he and not they would be responsible for the consequences. I was also informed by the same party that the officer to whom the note was addressed, on reading it, threw it on the floor, rubbing it under his foot and bade the bearer to go and tell Quantrell and his outlaws to go to Hades and do their worst.

The bearer of this note, so I was told, was a Frenchman who had lived in this country for some years but had never taken the oath of allegiance to our government. When the war between the North [and] South broke out, he applied and obtained through the French Minister at Washington City, such papers as were necessary for his protect[ion] as a citizen of France.

167

Quantrell, knowing this, forced him under the threat of death and the utter destruction of his property, to bear his note to the Federal Officer at this place. However, the story of the note, true or false, with the facts before us as I have stated them without bias or color, we are forced to the conclusion that beyond a doubt the falling of the building in which the wives and sisters of some of Quantrell's men were incarcerated, led to the Lawrence Massacre.

And now, assuring all who have listened so patiently to my story of that dreadful tragedy, that not one line has been dictated by prejudice or colored by misrepresentation, I close my paper on my "Recollections of Old Times in Kansas City."

Transcribed August 2009
Updated March 2011
by David W. Jackson
Archives and Education Director
Jackson County Historical Society
Independence, Missouri

BIBLIOGRAPHIC NOTES

The process of gathering together the documentation to reconstruct Mattie's life mirrors the making of a quilt. First, I had to find the scraps, remnants and new discoveries which lay scattered throughout family keepsakes, stories and records, local histories, censuses, historical and genealogical archives. Once I had assembled the surviving pieces of her story, I had to trim and shape them into a pattern of quilt blocks representing the overall shape of who she was and what she did. A simple recitation of her life events could not adequately communicate the meaning of her actions and choices. To more fully understand this compelling woman's life, the quilt blocks had to be set together within the context of the culture and community in which she lived, which turned my attention to the history and cultural attitudes of the time. For readers who wish to read or research some of the material I accessed, I include these references.

Bloch, E. Maurice. *George Caleb Bingham: A Catalogue Raisonne*. Berkeley, California: University of California Press, 1967.

Brackman, Barbara. *Borderland in Butternut and Blue: A Sampler Quilt to Recall the Civil War along the Kansas Missouri Border*. Kansas City: Kansas City Star Books, 2007.

Brown, A(ndrew) Theodore. *Frontier Community: Kansas City to 1870*. Columbia, Missouri: University of Missouri Press, 1963.

Case, Theodore Spencer, ed. *History of Kansas City, Missouri with Illustrations and Biographical Sketches of Some of Its Prominent Men and Pioneers*. Syracuse, New York: D. Mason and Company, 1888.

Constant, Alberta Wilson. *Paintbox on the Frontier: The Life and Times of George Caleb Bingham*. New York: Crowell Publishers, 1974.

Deatherage, Charles P. E*arly History of Greater Kansas City, Missouri & Kansas: the Prophetic City at the Mouth of the Kaw*. Diamond Jubilee Edition. Kansas City, Missouri, 1927, i.e., 1928.

Findlen, Rose Ann. *Borderland Families—Always on the Edge: Journey of the Lykins, Peery and Heiskell Familes along the Missouri and Kansas Border.* Published by Generations Books through On-Demand Publishing, LLC, DBA createspace.com, 2011.

German-American Biographical Publishing Company. *Kansas City und sein Deutschthum im 19. Jahrhundert.* Cleveland, Ohio: German-American Biographical Publishing Company, 1900.

Gilmore, Donald. *Civil War on the Missouri-Kansas Border.* Gretna, Louisiana: Pelican Publishing Company, 2006.

Goodrich, Thomas. *Black Flag: Guerilla Warfare on the Western Border, 1861-1865: A Riveting Account of a Bloody Chapter in Civil War History.* Bloomington: Indiana University Press, 1999.

Goodrich, Thomas. *Bloody Dawn: The Story of the Lawrence Massacre.* Kent, Ohio and London, England: The Kent State University Press, 1991.

Goodrich, Thomas. *War to the Knife: Bleeding Kansas 1854-1861.* Lincoln: University of Nebraska Press, 1988.

Hamilton, Jean Tyree, "Mr. Bingham's Tombstone," *Missouri Historical Review.* Columbia, Missouri: The State Historical Society of Missouri, ed. Richard S. Brownlee, Volume 1, no.1, July, 1979, 426-433.

Historic Kansas City Foundation. "Graffiti Gives Notice to Lykins House," *Gazette* 1989 (July-August), 1, 8.

Honig, Louis O. *Westport: Gateway to the Early West.* It Happened in America Series: Subscribers' Edition ([Kansas City?], Missouri, 1950).

Mattie Lykins' Scrapbook, microfilm in Dr. Johnston Lykins (1800-1876) and Martha Lykins Bingham (1824-1890) Collection, KC-0294; Native Sons of Greater Kansas City Archives, State Historical Society of Missouri Research Center-Kansas City, Kansas City, Missouri.

Nagel, Paul C. *George Caleb Bingham: Missouri's Famed Painter and Forgotten Politician.* Columbia, Missouri: University of Missouri Press, 2005.

Petersen, Paul R. and David W. Jackson. *Lost Souls of the Lost Township: Untold Life Stories of the People Buried in the Davis-Smith Cemetery, Kansas City, Jackson County, Missouri*. Kansas City, Missouri: The Orderly Pack Rat, 2011.

Rafiner, Tom A. *Caught Between Three Fires: Cass County, Missouri, Chaos, & Order No. 11, 1860-1865*. Bloomington, Indiana: Xlibris Corporation, 2010.

Stone, Jeffrey C. *Slavery, Southern Culture, and Education in Little Dixie, Missouri, 1820-1860*. New York and London: Routledge Press Series' Studies in African American History and Culture, Ed. Graham Hodges, Colgate University, 2006.

Whitney, Carrie Westlake. *Kansas City, Missouri: Its History and Its People, 1808-1908*, Vol 1. Chicago: The S.J. Clarke Publishing Company, 1908.

ILLUSTRATIONS

Front Cover

Missouri Star
Jeanne Poore, Overland Park, Kansas, "The Missouri Star Block, Butternut and Blue," quilted by Beth Dawson in *Borderland in Butternut and Blue: A Sampler Quilt to Recall the Civil War Along the Kansas/Missouri Border*, Barbara Brackman. Kansas City Star Books, 2007, 119. Used with permission of Kansas City Star Books, Kansas City, Missouri.

"Mrs. General Bingham" (attributed). See description for image 105.

Chapter 1

10. "The Map of the Western Rivers, 1842," used with permission of The Wisconsin Historical Society, Madison, Wisconsin, Image number WHi-80819. Cropped to show the Missouri River from Independence to Jefferson City.

11. "Historical View of Missouri's State Capitol in 1842," used with permission of Missouri State Archives, Jefferson City, Missouri.

12. "A New Map of Kentucky with Insets Showing Lexington, the Falls of Ohio, and the Ohio River, 1847," used with permission of The Wisconsin Historical Society, Madison, Wisconsin, Image number WHi-80593. Cropped to show Mattie's ancestral homeland.

13. "Little Dixie, Missouri," Missouri Division-Southern Division of the Confederacy. www.missouridivision-svc.org/litdixmap.htm.

15. Handwritten Excerpt from "*The Forest Cottage*;" Mattie Lykins' Scrapbook, np, Dr. Johnston Lykins (1800-1876) and Martha Lykins Bingham (1824-1890) Collection, KC-0294; Native Sons of Greater Kansas City Archives, State Historical Society of Missouri Research Center-Kansas City, Kansas City, Missouri.

16. Section of Martha Ann Livingston's "Mary Sharp," *Shelby News*, Shelbyville, Kentucky, 1840. Mattie Lykins'Scrapbook, np, Dr. Johnston Lykins (1800-1876) and Martha Lykins Bingham (1824-1890) Collection, KC-0294; Native Sons of Greater Kansas City Archives, State Historical Society of Missouri Research Center-Kansas City, Kansas City, Missouri.

Chapter 2

19. Martha Ann "Mattie" (Livingston) Lykins photograph by S.M. Eby & Son, Ambrotype and Photographic Artists, Kansas City, Missouri, 1865 (the only year S. M. Eby & Son were listed in annual Kansas City city directories, at the corner of 3rd and Main Streets, 3rd floor). One undated newspaper clipping claimed that Mattie was the first woman to have a photo made in Kansas City. In March 2011, Mr. Robert Dewit Owen, a great-great grandnephew of Mattie, donated this original image to the Jackson County Historical Society, Independence, Missouri, where it accompanies his previous gift of Mattie's original, "Recollections of Old Times in Kansas City," and unpublished manuscripts of his grandmother, Mrs. Dewit Livingston (Ada Campbell) Owen. (JCHS01315M)

20. Johnston Lykins. Portrait by George Caleb Bingham, and used with permission of Bingham-Waggoner Historical Society, 313 West Pacific Avenue, Independence, Missouri. This portrait is on long-term loan to the Society by the Native Sons and Daughters of Kansas City.

24. "Early Kansas City, 1855," in Carrie Westlake Whitney, *Kansas City, Missouri: Its History and Its People, 1808-1908, Vol 1* (Chicago: The S.J. Clarke Publishing Company, 1908), 126.

27. "Great Bend in the Missouri River at Kansas City from an Old Print," in Carrie Westlake Whitney, *Kansas City, Missouri: Its History and Its People, 1808-1908, Vol 1* (Chicago: The S.J. Clarke Publishing Company, 1908), 213.

29. Editor's Note from *The Western Metropolitan*, Kansas City, Missouri, regarding "*The Twin Sisters*, or "*The Scattered Household*;" Mattie Lykins' Scrapbook, np, Dr. Johnston Lykins (1800-1876) and Martha Lykins Bingham (1824-1890) Collection, KC-0294; Native Sons of Greater Kansas City Archives, State Historical Society of Missouri Research Center-Kansas City, Kansas City, Missouri.

30. "*The Two Orphans,*" and "*Twin Sisters,*" two of Mattie's romances; Mattie Lykins' Scrapbook, np, Dr. Johnston Lykins (1800-1876) and Martha Lykins Bingham (1824-1890) Collection, KC-0294; Native Sons of Greater Kansas City

Archives, State Historical Society of Missouri Research Center-Kansas City, Kansas City, Missouri.

34. "Old Gillis House," in Carrie Westlake Whitney, *Kansas City, Missouri: Its History and Its People, 1808-1908, Vol 1* (Chicago: The S.J. Clarke Publishing Company, 1908), 131.

38. Martha Ann "Mattie" (Livingston) Lykins, "Home for the Orphans of Confederate Soldiers," *The Kansas City* (Mo.) *Star*, 24 July 1927.

39. "Gully town" created when the bluffs rising on the south bank of the Missouri River were lowered. Watkins Bank is on the right. Mechanics Bank is on the left. They flank Second Street in this view looking east toward Main Street. Theodore Spencer Case (1832-1900) Collection, KC-0295; Native Sons of Greater Kansas City Archives, State Historical Society of Missouri Research Center-Kansas City, Kansas City, Missouri.

41. "William Gilpin's Prophetic, Map, 1859," in Carrie Westlake Whitney, *Kansas City, Missouri: Its History and Its People, 1808-1908, Vol 1* (Chicago: The S.J. Clarke Publishing Company, 1908), 667.

43. The Lykins Mansion on Quality Hill, "The Residence of Johnston Lykins," Charles P. Deatherage, *Early History of Greater Kansas City, Missouri & Kansas: the Prophetic City at the Mouth of the Kaw.* Diamond Jubilee Edition. (Kansas City, Missouri, 1927), 475.

44. "Sketch Map of Early Kansas City." Henry C. Haskell and Richard B. Fowler, *City of the Future: A Narrative History of Kansas City, 1850-1950* (Kansas City, Missouri: Frank Glenn Publishing, 1950), endpapers.

Chapter 3

49. "Fort Union, 1861," in Carrie Westlake Whitney, *Kansas City, Missouri: Its History and Its People, 1808-1908, Vol 1* (Chicago: The S.J. Clarke Publishing Company, 1908), 201. According to Coates, *In Memoriam, "Camp Union, as the barracks were styled by Major R. T. Van Horn, was located in the vicinity of 10th and Central Streets. It was build from June 20th to July...1861, and was about 200 feet square, fronting on 10th Street." In Memoriam, facing page 186. The structure to the right are the "Coates House foundations laid in 1860; boarded over and used for cavalry barns," 56, 57.*

50. "The Missouri-Kansas Border, 1860-1865," from *Civil War on the Missouri-Kansas Border* by Donald L. Gilmore ©2005 used by permission of the publisher, Pelican Publishing Company, Inc.

54. "Civil War Loyalties Within Mattie's Circle," graphic designed by author/graphically created by David W. Jackson.

61. Although the exact building in this block of buildings was not identified in the photo caption as the Union Jail in downtown Kansas City, it was one of these on the "east side of Grand Avenue, between 14th and 15th Streets." View looking north from 15th Street. Courtesy of the Jackson County Historical Society Archives, Independence, Missouri, JCHS000725L.

63. *Harper's Weekly*, 5 Sept 1863. Egraving titled, "The Destruction of the City of Lawrence, Kansas, and the Massacre of its Inhabitants by the Rebel Guerillas, August 21, 1863," page 564. A short article titled, "The Massacre at Lawrence, Kansas," about the atrocities of William Clarke Quantrill, follows on page 566. Courtesy Jackson County Historical Society.

64. *Harper's Weekly*, 19 Sept 1863. This issue includes an engraving on p. 604 titled, "The Ruins of Lawrence, Kansas." A short article titled, "The Destruction of Lawrence, Kansas," preecedes on page 603. Courtesy Jackson County Historical Society.

70. "Martial Law," or "Order No. 11," by George Caleb Bingham, from an original, antique photograph of the painting taken by Kansas City photographer, W. T. Dole. Courtesy of Jackson County Historical Society, JCHS004009L.

74-78. List of Persons Banished from Kansas City by Special Order No. 64, 29 August 1863, Union Provost Marshal's File of Papers Relating to Two or More Civilians, microcopy 416, Missouri State Archives, Jefferson City, Missouri.

80. Thomas Nast engraving, "Life of a Spy." Courtesy of Washington University Libraries, Department of Special Collecitons, St. Louis, Missouri.

81. "Old McGee Hotel," in Carrie Westlake Whitney, *Kansas City, Missouri: Its History and Its People, 1808-1908, Vol 1* (Chicago: The S.J. Clarke Publishing Company, 1908), 99.

Chapter 4

89. Confederate Widows' and Orphans' Home, 1867; Mattie Lykins' Scrapbook, np, Dr. Johnston Lykins (1800-1876) and Martha Lykins Bingham (1824-1890) Collection, KC-0294; Native Sons of Greater Kansas City Archives, State Historical Society of Missouri Research Center-Kansas City, Kansas City, Missouri.

92. "The Waif Left at the State Line House," *Kansas City Times,"* Mattie Lykins' Scrapbook, np, Dr. Johnston Lykins (1800-1876) and Martha Lykins Bingham (1824-1890) Collection, KC-0294; Native Sons of Greater Kansas City Archives, State Historical Society of Missouri Research Center-Kansas City, Kansas City, Missouri.

93. *"The Orphans' Advocate,"* August, 1872; Mattie Lykins' Scrapbook, np, Dr. Johnston Lykins (1800-1876) and Martha Lykins Bingham (1824-1890) Collection, KC-0294; Native Sons of Greater Kansas City Archives, State Historical Society of Missouri Research Center-Kansas City, Kansas City, Missouri.

93." *The Orphan*" and *"Acknowledgments;"* Mattie Lykins' Scrapbook, np, Dr. Johnston Lykins (1800-1876) and Martha Lykins Bingham (1824-1890) Collection, KC-0294; Native Sons of Greater Kansas City Archives, State Historical Society of Missouri Research Center-Kansas City, Kansas City, Missouri.

95. *"Appeal of Orphans' Home Society,"* April 1873; Mattie Lykins' Scrapbook, np, Dr. Johnston Lykins (1800-1876) and Martha Lykins Bingham (1824-1890) Collection, KC-0294; Native Sons of Greater Kansas City Archives, State Historical Society of Missouri Research Center-Kansas City, Kansas City, Missouri.

96. "The Gillham Road Change," *Kansas City* (Mo.) *Star,* 23 Aug. 1900. For more information, see, "Turned to Childish Treble," *Kansas City* (Mo.) *Times,* 8 Dec. 1889, 20.

98. German-American Biographical Publishing Company. *Kansas City und sein Deutschthum im 19. Jahrhundert.* Cleveland, Ohio: German-American Biographical Publishing Company, 1900, 40.

99. "The Journal, 13 Mar 1874, newspaper story on the completion of the Orphan Home; Mattie Lykins' Scrapbook, Dr. Johnston Lykins (1800-1876) and Martha Lykins Bingham (1824-1890) Collection, KC-0294; Native Sons of Greater Kansas

City Archives, State Historical Society of Missouri Research Center-Kansas City, Kansas City, Missouri.

100. Mr. Jaudon's hand is resting on the copper box which was found empty. The location is south of 31st Street and west of Gillham Road. According to an article in The Kansas City Star, July 24, 1927, the cornerstone was a large block of Carroll County blue limestone. Apparently the copper box had been opened at some point earlier by unknown persons and the contents removed. The newspaper article lists what was originally placed in it. If there had been any contents found, the items were to have gone to the Kansas City Historical Society. Photo courtesy of Missouri Valley Special Collections, Kansas City Public Library, Kansas City, Missouri, P1, General Collection, Charitable Organizations- -Little Sisters of the Poor, #3, Bar Code 10023028.

102. Lykins Mansion, *Kansas City* (Mo.) *Star*, 2 Aug. 1942.

102. Inset. The Lykins Mansion on Quality Hill, "The Residence of Johnston Lykins," Charles P. Deatherage, E*arly History of Greater Kansas City, Missouri & Kansas: the Prophetic City at the Mouth of the Kaw*. Diamond Jubilee Edition. (Kansas City, Missouri, 1927), 475.

103. "Graffiti gives notice to Lykins House," Historic Kansas City Foundation, *Gazette* 1989 (July/August)13:3, 1, 8.

104. George Caleb Bingham, American (1811-1879). *Self-Portrait*, ca. 1877. Oil on canvas, 27 1/16 x 22 1/16 inches (95.9 x 82.9 cm). The Nelson-Atkins Museum of Art, Kansas City, Missouri. Lent by the Kansas City Public Library, 1-1955. Photoreproduction by John Lamberton.

105. "*Mrs. General Bingham*" (attributed) (currently identified as "*An Unknown Woman*"). Oil portrait strongly favoring the likeness of Martha Ann "Mattie" (Livingston) Lykins Bingham, and in the painting style of George Caleb Bingham.
    This unframed, 36 x 24 inches painting was purchased by Dr. Kathryn McGonigal around 2000 from a reputable dealer in Herman, Missouri, who had previously purchased it at auction in St. Louis. Its provenance prior to this is undocumented.
    It is known that a Bingham painting of "*Mrs. General Bingham*" was sold at an estate auction in 1893, in Higginsville, Missouri, where it, "may possibly be identified with one of 'five family portraits,' included in inventory of the artist's estate, September, 1879 (no. 12); in administrator's sale of the Bingham estate, Findlay's Art Store, Kansas City, Missouri, March 25, 1893. (Bloch, 156-157).

At this printing, this oil portrait is in a private collection. Art historians and Bingham scholars are currently studying this portrait in an attempt to authenticate it as Mrs. Bingham, likely in mourning after the death of her first husband, Dr. Johnston Lykins, and possibly created as a companion to Bingham's ca. 1877 "Self-Portrait."

The author wishes to thank the present owner for allowing this promising portrait to debut in print in *Missouri Star*.

106. Monument marking the grave of George Caleb Bingham at Union Cemetery, Kansas City, Missouri. Photo courtesy of the State Historical Society of Missouri.

109. Martha Ann "Mattie" (Livingston) Lykins Bingham. "Home for the Orphans of Confederate Soldiers," *Kansas City* (Mo.) *Star*, 24 July 1927; and, "Helping Hand for Civil War Vanquished," by Frances Bush, *Kansas City* (Mo.) *Times*, 15 Aug. 1975.

Chapter 5

119. Two images, courtesy the author, of an 1835 manision in Frankfort, Kentucky. This is a home that Mattie would have been familiar with, and her future home in Kansas City, the Lykins mansion, was a near replica of this historic structure.

120. Franklin County Courthouse, postcard ca. 1907, courtesy Kentucky History Center, Frankfort, Kentucky.

128. Descendants of Stephen Livingston and Martha Jackson

Back Cover

Martha Ann "Mattie" (Livingston) Lykins Photograph by S.M. Eby & Son, Ambrotype and Photographic Artists, Kansas City, Missouri, 1865 (the **only** year S. M. Eby & Son were listed in annual Kansas City city directories, at the corner of 3rd and Main Streets, 3rd floor). Additional description is provided in the illustration used on page 19. (JCHS01315M)

D. June Ford, Overland Park, Kansas, 2004, "Butternut and Blue," quilted by Beth Dawson in *Borderland in Butternut and Blue: A Sampler Quilt to Recall the Civil War Along the Kansas/Missouri Border, Barbara Brackman*. Used with permission of Kansas City: Kansas City Star Books, 2007, 119.

COLOPHON

The main text of this book is in 12-point Garamond typeface, a true-type font, and designed using Microsoft Word 2007. Chapter heads and sub-heads are set in Californian FB, at 18pt boldface.

The author contracted independently with David W. Jackson, archivist for the Jackson County Historical Society, to design and lay-out this book using the author's original manuscript.

A transcript of Mattie Lykins Bingham's handwritten "*Recollections,*" was added in it entirety for reader's interest, and to make this important manuscript available to a wider audience, with gratitude to the donor, Mr. Robert Dewit Owen, in memory of his grandmother, Mrs. Dewit Livingston (Ada Campbell) Owen.

The author researched and secured image reproductions and permissions. Additional images were discovered and financed independently by Jackson.

Finally, Jackson created an index using Word's built-in indexing mark-up tools. Endnotes are set in 10pt Times New Roman, and the Index is in 10pt Garamond typeface.

The finalized Microsoft Word document was reformatted into Adobe Systems portable document format (pdf) format (viewed using Adobe Acrobat Reader), then transmitted electronically using file transfer protocol (ftp) to http://www.createspace.com. *CreateSpace* is a *DBA* (Doing Business As) of On-Demand Publishing LLC, part of the Amazon group of companies.

A cover was designed by Jackson using CreateSpace's online cover design tool.

The book was imprinted and assigned an ISBN through the Jackson County Historical Society, and is printed on-demand to a worldwide audience.

ABOUT THE JACKSON COUNTY
HISTORICAL SOCIETY

The Jackson County Historical Society is proud to have assisted Rose Ann Findlen in her research and commends her efforts to record and preserve the memory of the life and times of Mattie Lykins Bingham, widow of George Caleb Bingham. We also thank Findlen for sharing the proceeds from this inaugural biography of a fascinating woman.

Mattie Lykins Bingham and her second husband, the celebrated "Missouri Painter," have long been subjects of interest to the Jackson County Historical Society. The Society's founding and an early day celebration of the artist share a common year. In 1909, the Society held its earliest recorded gathering of over 200 for an Independence Day picnic on the lawn of the homestead of John B. Wornall, an esteemed pioneer of Jackson County. Later that year, in December, George Caleb Bingham's son, Rollins Bingham, loaned George Caleb Bingham's art for an exhibition assembled by the Fine Arts Institute and exhibited at the Duke Building in downtown Kansas City. The exhibition boasted more than 250 works of art valued at $200,000 ($4.7 million in 2009 dollars).

Rollins described this exhibition of his father's art as *"the life work of a Missouri artist. . . . Though small in numbers comparative to the abundance of his life work is completely and thoroughly representative of his best in each manner and kind of artistic expression to which, necessity, choice and circumstance in his whole career directed his talent."* Of all the artists represented, *The Kansas City Star* proclaimed, "from an historical point of view, the paintings by George Caleb Bingham are the most important."

183

Bingham's artistic and historical importance continues to be linked to the mission of the Jackson County Historical Society. The Society is proud to partner in the 2011 Bicentennial celebrating the birth of George Caleb Bingham, and prizes its original Sartain engraving of *Order No. 11*, signed by Bingham.

The Jackson County Historical Society collects historical documents, photographs, maps and books that record the people, places and events of today...and those of our ancestors. For more than 50 years the Society has made its holdings accessible to the public where they are housed in the historic Truman Jackson County Courthouse on Independence Square in Independence, Missouri.

The nonprofit organization still pursues its mission of preservation of the County's rich history. In addition to an Archives and Research Library, its museum, the 1859 Jail and Marshal's Home, is an authentic relic of Jackson County's earliest days.

The Society welcomes your inquiries on how you may support its mission, collections, and activities.

ACKNOWLEDGMENTS

This book certainly didn't get written all by itself. The coverlet we have quilted for Mattie involved the loving work of a number of people. David W. Jackson, Director of Archives and Education for the Jackson County Historical Society, applied his knowledge of the history and architecture of Kansas City to enrich the story of Mattie's life and times. By day, his vigorous pursuit of images and their stories, and his interactions with scholars and archivists in his professional community facilitated the use of a myriad of sources. At night, he still had creativity and energy left to create the interior layout and cover design for *Missouri Star*. Perhaps when he slept—if he did—he dreamed about the possibilities for this book.

Robert Dewit Owen, Mattie's great-great grandnephew, has generously shared his family treasures and his knowledge of Mattie and her extended family to make them available to historical and genealogical researchers for generations to come. Larry Livingston, a descendant of William Jackson Livingston, shared records from his family Bible and provided valuable genealogical and historical information to help round out the story of Mattie's brother and his descendants.

Dr. Kathryn McGonigal's graciousness in leading us to obtaining an image of the painting purported to be Bingham's "*Mrs. General Bingham*" gives the reader an opportunity to imagine how this spirited pioneer may have appeared to her newlywed husband, George Caleb Bingham. The viewing of this image provides a rich opportunity for Bingham scholars to consider the authentication of the painting.

My husband, George Findlen, took countless hours away from his own research and writing to bring this book to fruition. He enhanced, critiqued and formatted the complex genealogical details, even taking time out to create delicious dinners for his wife so that she could continue to write.

Rose Ann Findlen

ABOUT THE AUTHOR

Rose Ann (Gard) Wallace Findlen grew up on a farm in the Missouri-Kansas Borderland with little awareness of the region's history as the place where critical issues shaping the nation's destiny came together in nineteenth century America: the abolition of slavery, the continued subjugation of the American Indian, and Western expansion. Following her graduation from Northwest Missouri State University, she moved to Lawrence, Kansas, to pursue graduate studies in English at the University of Kansas.

In Lawrence, her newfound Kansas friends pointed out the Eldridge Hotel [not to be confused with the Eldridge Hotel in Kansas City, also known as the Gilliss House Hotel], built on the site of the original hotel burned in Quantrill's Raid, and suggested that her little house on Vermont Street must have been built shortly after the raid. Beyond that, she had only a passing interest in the history of the region, but if the author had known about Mattie Lykins at that time, she would have been entranced by the compassionate, brave, spirited (sometimes misguided) woman.

Living in France and the former Yugoslavia, teaching English to Native Americans in Colorado, providing courses to soldiers monitoring communiqués across the Iron Curtain, finishing a Ph.D., becoming a mother and a college English professor filled Findlen's mind and her time. Only after a career in college administration, in which she served as dean, provost, and president, did she turn seriously to writing and to looking at the history of the region where she had grown up.

Through her research and writing, Findlen came to appreciate the impact of the historical events of the nineteenth century on the generations of Missourians and Kansans to follow.

Issues of individual and states' rights versus federal priorities, race relations, and economic and cultural values in the two states flamed into regional conflict just prior to the Civil War but continue on a national level today.

As the author studied Mattie and her contemporaries, she grew in her appreciation of Mattie, her friends, and her family as each and all of them struggled to find a way forward that would sustain them and preserve everything they had worked for. The author hopes the reader will also come to appreciate these fore bearers whose struggles so closely resemble our own.

Rose Ann Findlen is the author of *Borderland Families Always on the Edge,* a saga of Missouri and Kansas pioneers.

INDEX

191

Jackson County Historical Society
P.O. Box 4241
Independence, MO 64051
(816) 252-7454
jchs.org
info@jchs.org

www.ingramcontent.com/pod-product-compliance
Lightning Source LLC
Chambersburg PA
CBHW060749050426
42449CB00008B/1335